PRESTON HOLLOW

PRESTON HOLLOW

· A BRIEF HISTORY ·

JACK WALKER DRAKE

FOREWORD BY MARK CUBAN

THE
History
PRESS

Published by The History Press
Charleston, SC
www.historypress.com

Images courtesy of the author unless otherwise noted.

First published 2021

Manufactured in the United States

ISBN 9781467149389

Library of Congress Control Number: 2021938376

This book is dedicated to all those who contributed. To the Dilbeck owners, thank you for letting me wander through your house with a camera! Your houses are so special and mean so much to this neighborhood. Thank you again for preserving this amazing architecture. To the 1920s homeowners, your homes' stories are so unique—thank you for letting me showcase them for the book! To the people who allowed me to photograph your houses, thank you! I know it's random to receive a letter in the mail from a person asking to have a picture of your house for a book.

To all the longtime residents with whom I spoke, your stories are so amazing, and I'm so glad they were included. And most importantly, special thanks to my family for supporting me and encouraging me throughout the process. Thank you to everyone who trusted a fifteen-year-old to write a book.

CONTENTS

FOREWORD

I remember when I first drove through Preston Hollow. I was living with five roommates in a three-bedroom apartment in The Village on Shadybrook Lane. Not a far distance from Preston Hollow in miles, but aspirationally, it seemed a lifetime away. Then one day, driving around looking at houses—with my company succeeding beyond my wildest dreams—I took a turn down a bumpy street and saw a "For Sale" sign at 8500 Jourdan Way. It wasn't the biggest house or the prettiest, and to be honest it was run-down. But it had over an acre of land. Having a big yard was always a dream of mine and to find 1.8 acres within the Dallas city limits seemed too good to be true. The price was a little out of my range, but I had always read that you should buy the worst house in the best neighborhood, so I did. I bought a house in Preston Hollow. It was a dream come true and started a thirty-year love affair with Preston Hollow. It's my favorite part of Dallas and always will be.

—Mark Cuban

INTRODUCTION

Today, the neighborhood of Preston Hollow is arguably one of the most desirable in Dallas. West of Preston Road, large estates stand on lots acres in size with thousands of one-hundred-year-old trees towering high above their massive homes. East of Preston, many original two-story homes and single-story ranch-style homes still stand from the 1930s and 1940s, while others have been demolished to make way for newer homes twice their size. Dave Perry-Miller Reality describes Preston Hollow as being "renowned for its tree-lined streets, winding 'country' roads and beautifully built pre-War and new homes on wooded lots." Its proximity to world-class shopping and dining, as well as Dallas's most elite private schools and country clubs, has long attracted Dallas's most affluent residents. Originally, the lull of rural country living located just minutes from the city attracted the attention of wealthy investors, developers and businessmen. Today, a leisurely drive down the long blocks bordered with hackberry, oak and pecan trees will give one the feeling of being transported to another time and place.

However, it didn't start this way. Early settlers established large family farms in the mid-1800s. It wasn't until the 1920s that people began purchasing property for residential use. The first to do so was Ralph Benjamin Stichter, credited with building the first pair of houses not associated with farm use in the neighborhood, one for himself and one for his son. His legacy was followed by Ira Pleasant DeLoache and Al Joyce, both of whom turned Preston Hollow's farmland into blocks of houses. Famous architects, like Charles Dilbeck, built estates in early

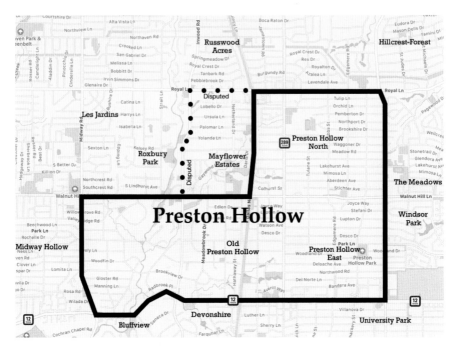

A present-day map of Preston Hollow.

Preston Hollow. Being only six to seven miles from downtown Dallas, many would say this is the perfect distance to work, but in the 1850s, these six to seven miles led you to the country. Almost nothing existed north of downtown Dallas.

Chapter 1

THE ORIGINAL SETTLERS

1856–1923

Growing up on a dairy was work, work. And after that more work to be done. Cows milked twice a day seven days a week; milk put in glass bottles and delivered house to house every day. Then all the farming to be done growing feed for the cattle. No way one could ever get caught up it seemed. The income was small but there was always food on the table. It was a hard life but it was a good life.
—Jack Lively Jr., grandson of dairy farmer John Lively, one of the first settlers in Preston Hollow

Dallas wasn't near what it is today in the mid-1800s. In 1848, Dallas had fewer than 50 residents, with that number jumping to 500 by 1860. Despite the city being so small, 8,665 residents—made up of mostly farmers and their farmhands—lived in Dallas County. Stagecoach services connected the town to nearby cities like Fort Worth or even to Santa Fe. Residents of Dallas wanted modern transportation to reach their city, and they had lost hope in seeing a railroad connection in the near future since the Civil War caused the Houston and Texas Central Railroad to halt its plans to expand to North Texas. Leaders of Dallas saw the Trinity River as their only possibility for a connection to the outside world and offered James H. McGarvey and Dick Dowling $15,000 to captain a boat from Galveston to Dallas in May 1867. The expedition took an entire year! In 1872, the Houston and Texas Central Railroad resumed expansion plans, and the first locomotive arrived in Dallas on July 16, 1872. A huge five-hundred-table barbecue celebration followed. This event, as well as the Texas and Pacific

Railroad arriving a year later, helped shape Dallas into what it is today. However, even with the population of Dallas rapidly growing, very little was happening six miles to the north.

The first known settler to move to what is now Preston Hollow was Jesse Meaders in the 1850s. His son, James, took over the land. The Meaders family owned 320 acres of land north of Walnut Hill and west of Hillcrest. Jesse built a farmhouse near Meaders Lane in 1856. Others shortly followed. The Howell family was granted land from Governor Elisha M. Pease in 1857, but they quickly started selling off portions of their 546 acres to other settlers. The Wright family, descendants of John Howell, owned much of the land that is now Old Preston Hollow. Around that same time, Patrick Henry Lively also received a large land grant, the western part of Preston Hollow and the northern part of Bluffview. He built a farmstead located on Guernsey Lane in the 1870s. Following his early death, his wife, Laura, and son, John Thompson Lively, managed the farm. After the First World War, John and his son, Jack Lively Sr., began operating what was called the Bluff View Dairy. John Jackson owned the land from about Park Lane to Walnut Hill to Edgemere to Hillcrest. The Jackson family owned this land until after World War II. The Caruth family owned much of the land that would become University Park and most likely portions of eastern Preston Hollow. Hugh E. Prather owned the sliver of land south of Northwood Road and east of Preston, as well as other slivers of land. The Freemans owned much land in western Preston Hollow and even parts of Bluffview. In the 1910s, the St. Louis Southwestern Railway, also known as the Cotton Belt, laid railroad tracks through the area and built a station at what is now Meaders and the Dallas North Tollway, adding a connection to downtown Dallas other than Preston Road.

A painting of the original Lively farmhouse on Guernsey Lane. *Jack Lively*.

Ralph Stichter Sr.'s estate at Preston and Walnut Hill in September 1933. *St. Mark's School of Texas.*

In the early 1920s, a very wealthy man purchased property in Preston Hollow, but this time for a different intention than farming. His name was Ralph Benjamin Stichter. Born on April 18, 1876, to Franklin and Emma Stichter in Pike County, Missouri, Ralph Stichter would work his way up to becoming the general manager for the Denison-Sherman interurban line, later called the Texas Electric Railway system. He and his wife, Maude Stichter, wanted to move out to the country but still live on desirable land, so he purchased many acres of land northeast of Preston and Walnut Hill. He built two homes on his property: his estate, at the corner of Preston and Walnut Hill, and a home for his son, R.B. Stichter Jr., at what is now the corner of Lakehurst and Tulane. The home on Lakehurst was a gift to his son and his daughter-in-law, Mary Stichter, as a wedding present. When Ralph Stichter Sr. died from a bullet wound in 1932, Ralph Stichter Jr. and Mary Stichter moved into the estate on Walnut Hill, and their old home on Lakehurst was leased out for other uses. The home at Preston and Walnut Hill was demolished in 1961, with the location now part of the campus of Preston Hollow Presbyterian Church, but his son's original home is still standing at 6126 Lakehurst. The structure at that address is considered the first true home built in Preston Hollow, meaning it was not associated with a farm.

In 1922, something else monumental happened: a flight over Preston Hollow made by none other than Ira Pleasant DeLoache. Originally from North Hampton County, North Carolina, he sold tobacco in Wisconsin before moving to Dallas to work for the American Tobacco Company until 1915, when he switched to real estate. In 1924, he successfully developed his mother and father-in-law's land near Lubbock into the town of Whiteface, but then he decided to return to the beautiful land he had flown over two years prior.

Chapter 2

THE DELOACHE ERA

1924–1938

Half of…Preston Hollow is in high, rolling, black land prairie and the other half comprises beautiful wooded tracts, some of which have deep ravines with trickling picturesque brooks and small pools stocked with fish.
—*"Rural Home Sites in Preston Hollow," advertisement from 1926*

Similar to Ralph Stichter, Ira P. DeLoache saw the hidden beauty of Preston Hollow's land and decided that it could be developed for residential purposes. After his success in developing Whiteface, he purchased a fifty-six-acre farm at the northwest corner of Preston and Northwest Highway in 1924 to be developed, establishing this as the birth year of Preston Hollow. This area would be called Preston Downs. He built his residence on the land that is now 5950 Deloache Avenue, but his home had a Preston Road street address. Two years later, in 1926, he built a real estate office at the northwest corner of Preston and Northwest Highway. His office, which was also supposedly his carriage house, would later turn into the Preston Hollow town hall. Known as the "Little White House," it currently serves as an office for Ebby Halliday Realtors. Albert Joyce purchased many acres of land west of the Cotton Belt for future development. All the land west of Preston Road was intended to be developed into country-style estates on at least an acre of land. Many sit on creeks or ponds.

Despite DeLoache and Joyce buying up land in the early 1920s, very few homes were built until the late 1920s. Some other homes that were built in the neighborhood before DeLoache and Joyce's development include Stichter's

Ebby's Little White House was once Preston Hollow's town hall and Ira P. DeLoache's real estate office.

pair of homes on Preston and Walnut Hill (1922; demolished in 1961) and 6126 Lakehurst (1922); Captain E. Dick Slaughter's home: 5025 Lakehill Court (1922; demolished in 2019); 6331 Meadow, original owners unknown (1923; demolished in 2020); Albert Jackson's home at 4838 Walnut Hill, current address 9950 Strait Lane (1926); and the dairy farm at 6303 Meadow (1927). Another older home, which was part of a farm, was located near the intersection of Douglas and DeLoache. However, not much information about it survives. DeLoache and Joyce's development ultimately began in 1928, when the Thatchers built their now demolished home on Park Lane. Other early Preston Hollow residents included the William Harris family at 5111 Park Lane (1928); Chas P. Freeman at 9201 Meadowbrook (1928; demolished in 2012); Walker E. Jackson at 5520 Park Lane (1929); Nathan Wohlfeld at 6207 Glendora (1929); George L. Dexter at 9823 Preston (1929); Dan Bell at 4644 Park Lane (1930; demolished in about 2014); John Desco at 5931 Desco (1930); 6026 Mimosa (1930; demolished in 2009); Jim Wilcox at 8505 Douglas (1931; demolished in 2017);* Clay Pearce at 5722 Chatham Hill (1931); and Dr. Rubin Jackson at 5823 Deloache (1931; demolished in

---

* The house stood for many years on the Northwest Bible campus adjacent to their building. It was demolished in 2017, and a beach volleyball court stands in its place.

5200 Park Lane (1939) sits on 1.39 acres of land.

1978). Another home, at 9700 Inwood, was also built in 1929; however, the original owners are unknown.

In the late 1920s and the early 1930s, no restaurants or retail existed in Preston Hollow, the area that was originally known as the Preston Road District. In fact, even the trees didn't exist! DeLoache, along with Al Joyce, paid a crew one dollar for every hackberry tree they dug up along the Cotton Belt railroad and moved into the neighborhood. They also planted many oak and pecan trees. Many of these trees still line the streets of Preston Hollow. Al Joyce, a resident of Highland Park, developed the land west of the tracks and south of Park Lane into large estates that are included in today's "Old Preston Hollow." Longtime Preston Hollow resident Jim Williams said that the streets were gravel and remained that way until annexation. Electricity reached Preston Hollow in 1924. Telephone lines were scarce, and many families often shared one line, often referred to as "party lines." Richard Scurry remembers being able to pick up his phone and listen to his neighbors' conversations. He also remembers people asking one another to speed up their conversations so they could use the phone. Water was all well supplied until the homeowners formed a water district in 1930, led by

An old photo of Albert Jackson's home in Walnut Hill. *Lael Brodsky*.

DeLoache and Stichter. When city water reached Preston Hollow in 1931, a water tower was built at the southwest corner of Lakehurst and Edgemere, and Jim Williams remembers climbing the water tower as a child. City sewage did not exist; residents had septic tanks.

The residents of Preston Hollow would hunt and ride horses throughout the neighborhood. Many of the garages of the original homes were horse stables. Residents kept many other types of animals on their land as well. Former Preston Hollow resident Cindy Boswell Nienhueser, daughter of Hillcrest High School principal Fred Boswell, remembers riding horses through the streets of Preston Hollow North with W.C. "Dub" Miller, who owned a large estate near Lakehurst and the railroad and also owned a large collection of horses. The children would also fish in the ponds and play cowboys and Indians throughout the neighborhood. Barbara Fix, who lived on a 5.5-acre estate at the southeast corner of Inwood and Walnut Hill, remembers exploring and playing in the nearby creek. Marietta Scurry Johnson, who grew up and still lives on Winston Court, remembers playing all day in the neighborhood until her mom rang a cow bell to call her home for dinner. She also remembers putting coins on the Cotton Belt tracks and waiting for the train to flatten them. The neighborhood children would ride their horses to Highland Park and taunt the kids, betting them money that they couldn't ride. They would often win those bets! Jody Miller of Preston Hollow describes growing up in Preston Hollow as the "most delightful experience," adding that "I wish every child now could have as much fun as we had." Tom Dunning, who lived on Lakehurst, said that "for a kid, [Preston Hollow was] the neatest place in the world to live. There were lots of creeks to explore. I could ride my bicycle all over."

Elizabeth Dickey Mills's family kept many different types of animals on their estate at 9900 Preston. *Elizabeth Dickey Mills.*

In addition to riding the St. Louis Southwestern Railway (Cotton Belt), a bus service ran from downtown Dallas to the town of Roxbury Park via Douglas and Park Lane. Roxbury Park was a separate town located northwest of Walnut Hill (originally known as the Six Mile Lane) and Inwood on the streets of Kelsey, Dorset, North and South Lindhurst and so on. It was annexed by Dallas in 1945. Today, many people believe that the area bordered by Walnut Hill, Inwood, Royal and Midway is part of the Preston Hollow neighborhood; however, in actuality, that area does not fall within the official boundaries (see the map in the introduction for more details).

For public schooling, Preston Hollow kids, at first, attended Walnut Hill School (now Walnut Hill Elementary), which was west of Preston Hollow. The school was founded in 1914 at another location, and three acres of land were later acquired at the northwest corner of Walnut Hill and Midway; the current building was built in 1937. Jack Lively Sr. was one of four students in the original graduating class in 1916. Preston Hollow Elementary opened

Left: Cindy Boswell Nienhueser riding horses as a kid. *Cindy Boswell Nienhueser.*

Below: The Bowells built their second and bigger Preston Hollow house on their two acres in the late 1950s. Their first house, at 6135 Walnut Hill, was built in the 1940s. The Brock family lived to the west and also owned a large estate. The Brocks' house, which still stands, is at 6043 Walnut Hill Circle (1940). Their estate was split up into multiple lots to create Walnut Hill Circle in the 1980s.

Marietta Scurry Johnson's current and childhood home at 5542 Winston Court, built in 1935.

in the neighborhood during the 1945–46 school year. Hillcrest High School, formerly known as Vickery Meadows High School, opened in 1938 on land donated by the Caruth family as a joint school between Preston Hollow and Vickery, Texas, which was located to the east. For many years, kids were able to pay to attend Highland Park schools until the northern part of University Park (Villanova, Wentwood, Centenary, Marquette and more) was developed from 1948 into the 1950s and there was no longer space for Preston Hollow kids in the schools.

On March 15, 1932, Ralph Stichter, one of Preston Hollow's first residents, was shot in his yard. He passed away from his wounds later that day. His estate at Preston and Walnut Hill was given to his son, Ralph Stichter Jr., who moved in.

Founded in 1933, Texas Country Day School for Boys (TCD) opened as the first private school in Preston Hollow. The founders included Wirt Davis, Arthur Kramer, Elizabeth Penn, Hugo W. Schoellkopf and none other than Ira P. DeLoache. At the time, all of the founders had school-aged children. They did not want their children to attend public school,

Above: Hillcrest High School. *Elizabeth Dickey Mills.*

Left: Kenneth Bouve, headmaster of Texas Country Day School. *St. Mark's School of Texas.*

so they coaxed former educator Menter B. Terrill out of retirement to personally teach them. When Terrill retired for the second time, these parents rallied together to create their own private school. They established the Texas Country Day School for Boys and appointed Kenneth Bouve as the headmaster. It is rumored that for a very short period of time, classes were held at 6126 Lakehurst, the home originally built for Ralph Stichter Jr. by his father. Donald Allen, one of the first teachers at TCD, said, "I taught my first chemistry class of four students in a very tiny upstairs room in the garage." This possibly refers to the guest house, located above the garage, original to the property. In addition to leasing his original house on Lakehurst, Ralph Stichter Jr. later leased his gatehouse and ten acres of land at the northeast corner of Preston and Walnut Hill for playing fields to TCD. In September 1933, this larger location became its main campus. The gatehouse had three garages with two servants' quarters above, all of which were converted into a school building. Stichter's chicken house became the laboratory, while Mr. and Mrs. Bouve resided at 6126 Lakehurst. Classes were held from 8:30 a.m. to 5:00 p.m., with several breaks in between to hike and play sports on the fields and games in the streets of Preston Hollow North. In 1935, the school made additional improvements. It constructed another building for a study hall and two additional classrooms. A program was created for boarding students, and 6126 Lakehurst was converted into the dormitory. It was able to house eighteen students, who were charged $1,000 for boarding and schooling for one year. The school had almost fifty students that year, three of whom were boarding students.

During the early 1930s, wealthy businessmen continued to move into Preston Hollow, building luxe estates. The Tavenner "Tav" Lupton estate, built in 1934 at 9323 Preston Road, was one of the finest in Preston Hollow. Featuring a hand-dug swimming pool and guest houses, this home today sits on a 3.84-acre lot and is 16,100 square feet.

The lure of building large estates attracted famous architects, most notably Charles Dilbeck, who built monumental homes in Preston Hollow. Dilbeck's first Preston Hollow homes were the Peyton and Katherine Scrimshire house on 5234 Ravine, built in about 1933 (demolished), and the home of Edward James Solon, built in 1934 at the corner of Armstrong (now Douglas) and Averill Way (demolished). Born on May 27, 1909, in Fort Smith, Arkansas, Dilbeck always knew he wanted to be an architect. He attended two years of architectural school at Oklahoma State University, but he dropped out in 1929 and started his own architectural company. Dilbeck designed homes in Tulsa before moving to Dallas in 1933. He built homes in many parts of Dallas, but some of his best were built in Preston Hollow. He built many different styles of homes here. His earliest homes, like the Donald and Mary Anderson residence at 5252 Ravine (1935), featured his signature "crooked brick" and wood shingle roofs. Others, like Malcolm Cloyd's residence at 6122 Deloache (1938), were of French Normandy influence. Many examples of perhaps his most famous style, the Country Ranch, were built in Preston Hollow, ranging from smaller homes like the Metzger's residence at 6142 Walnut Hill (1946) to William Underwood's large estate at 5310 Park Lane (1938). Dilbeck always said, "A house should say, welcome, come right in, sit down and enjoy yourself." Author John Brooks Walton described Dilbeck's homes

Left: The Texas Country Day School Band in the 1930s. *St. Mark's School of Texas.*

Below: Students and faculty posing for a picture outside their school building. *St. Mark's School of Texas.*

as having "the Dilbeck signature of massive chimneys [and] tall window units opening into a vaulted ceiling living room, unusual patterns of stone and brick, and often a small turret at the front entrance." He added, "A Dilbeck house cries out, 'look at me, I am different from the rest.'" This is evident in Preston Hollow, where many Charles Dilbeck homes still stand. Anyone who is even somewhat familiar with Dilbeck's style can say, "That's a Dilbeck," when they drive by one of his homes. The Dilbeck homes remaining, from oldest to youngest, are 5252 Ravine (1935), 6315 Lakehurst (1935), 5500 Chatham Hill (1935), 9239 Hathaway (1937), 9506 Meadowbrook (1937), 5310 Park (1937), 6122 Deloache (1938), 6027 Glendora (1938), 6322 Northwood (1940), 5007 Deloache (1941), 6043 Park (1942), 5106 Deloache (1945), 6142 Walnut Hill (1946) and 6132 Deloache (1951). These homes, with both exterior and interior pictures, are featured in more detail in chapter 6. More homes are "rumored" to be Dilbecks; however, this cannot be proven.

6027 Glendora (1938) is one of Charles Dilbeck's works in Preston Hollow.

While the land to the west was being developed into large country estates, the land to the east of Preston was mainly being turned into single-story ranch-style houses; nonetheless, some two-stories were built on Deloache, Woodland, Desco, Mimosa, Lakehurst, Glendora, Meadow and Norway. Preston Hollow North's development commenced when Ralph Stichter sold off many of his acres beginning in 1928. Nathan Wholfeld, who had just emigrated from Poland, was the first to purchase a lot from Stichter in what was called "Preston Road Estates." He built his home at 6207 Glendora in 1929.

Development began in Preston Hollow East, originally called Preston Highlands, in the early to mid-1930s. Homebuilder Urie Jones constructed many houses there, most of which were single-story ranch homes. Urie Jones's flagship street was the 6000–6300 block of Deloache Avenue. These homes were all grand, exquisite two-story brick (or stone) homes, many of which are still standing. David and Holly Sudbury, who own the first house built on Woodland in 1935, say that "each [original house] was somehow individualized and charming," while also mentioning their "many great neighbors and verdant lots have truly made for a 'Wonderful Woodland.'"

One of Dilbeck's ornate but unique design touches was this brick pattern, seen on 6315 Lakehurst (1935).

This page: Many ranch-style homes like these two at 6138 Northwood (1940) and 6306 Northwood (1940) were built east of Preston Road.

6034 Meadow (1936).

Nathan Wholfeld's home at 6207 Glendora (1929).

This page: A family proudly stands by their new single-story ranch-style home under construction in the winter of 1937. *Jim Williams.*

6306 Deloache (1938) is one the homes on Urie Jones's flagship block. This home, both inside and outside, is being used as the set for Freeform's show *Cruel Summer*. *Debbie Tolson.*

6015 Woodland was the first house built on Woodland in 1935.

However, some lots in both Preston Hollow East and Preston Hollow North weren't built on until the late 1940s and early 1950s, especially those toward Hillcrest. The western part of Preston Hollow—bordered by Northwest Highway, Midway, Walnut Hill and Inwood—was owned by the Freeman and Lively families. After Mattie B. Freeman's husband's death in about 1932, she began selling her more than four hundred acres for development as an area called Sunnybrook Estates. The Lively family moved the dairy farm to 11200 Denton Drive in 1939–40, and their land was also developed. Jack Lively Jr., grandson of John Lively, remembers living on the farm before its relocation. The original homestead was demolished in the 1950s and split into two lots.

The largest boom of development took place from 1936 to 1940. At this point, most farmers and landholders had sold off their land for development, and moving into Preston Hollow was becoming popular. People in Dallas were tired of hefty city taxes, and many chose Preston Hollow over Highland Park because of what they described as a better sense of community and larger lots with no fences. Elizabeth Dickey Mills remembers her father,

6029 Northwood Road (1940) was owned by former president George W. Bush and Laura Bush from the 1980s until 1995, when they moved to the Governor's Mansion in Austin, Texas.

6214 Desco (1939).

Above and opposite: Jim Williams's childhood home at 3835 Kenmore Drive (now 6403 Mimosa) under construction in 1937. It was completed in 1938 and demolished in 1997. *Jim Williams.*

6315 Woodland (1940).

The Williams home after completion. Note how Mimosa was a gravel street. *Jim Williams.*

GF 4236 rd   *6402 MIMOSA   1938 - 1997*

EMPLOYERS CASUALTY COMPANY

━━━━ A Stock Company ━━━━ ━━━━━━━━━━━━ **DALLAS, TEXAS** ━━━━

Amount: $ 22,000.00

N? 612559

EMPLOYERS CASUALTY COMPANY, herein called the Company, for value does hereby guarantee to

W. B. WILLIAMS and wife, ROBBIE WILLIAMS,

herein styled insured, their heirs, executors and administrators, that they have good and indefeasible title to
the following described real property:

Situated in Dallas County, Texas, and being the West one-half of Lot One (1)
in Block Fifteen (15), of Preston Road Estates, an addition to the City of
Dallas, Dallas County, Texas, according to the Map thereof, recorded in
Volume 3, Page 298, of the Map Records of Dallas County, Texas,
subject to:

1. Following liens: Unpaid balance of one certain promissory note in the original
principal sum of $13,500.00, dated November 27, 1946, executed by Gustave
A. Valerius and wife, Betty A. Valerius, payable to the order of PHOENIX
MUTUAL LIFE INSURANCE COMPANY; said note being secured by vendor's lien re-
tained in deed of even date therewith, recorded in Volume 2757, Page 469,
of the Deed Records of Dallas County, Texas, and being further secured by
deed of trust of even date therewith executed by Gustave A. Valerius and
wife to OAKES T. TURNER, Trustee, recorded in Volume 1775, Page 283, of
the Deed of Trust Records of Dallas County, Texas

2. Restrictive covenants affecting the property above described.

3. Any discrepancies in area and boundaries which a correct survey would show.

4. Taxes for the current year.

Said Company shall not be liable in a greater amount than actual monetary loss of insured, and in no event shall said Company
be liable for more than TWENTY TWO THOUSAND AND NO/100 ($22,000.00) - - - - - - Dollars,
and shall, at its own cost, defend said insured in every suit or proceeding on any claim against or right to said land, or any part thereof,
adverse to the title hereby guaranteed, provided the party or parties entitled to such defense shall, within a reasonable time after the
commencement of such suit or proceeding, and in ample time for defense therein, give said Company written notice of the pendency
of the suit or proceeding, and authority to defend, and said Company shall not be liable until such adverse claim or right shall have
been held valid by a court of last resort to which either litigant may apply, and, if such adverse claim or right so established shall be
for less than the whole of the property then the liability of the Company shall be only such part of the whole liability limited above
as shall bear the same ratio to the whole liability that the adverse claim or right established may bear to the whole property. In the ab-
sence of notice as aforesaid, the Company is relieved from all liability with respect to such claim or demand; provided, however, that
failure to notify shall not prejudice the claim of the insured, if such insured shall not be a party to such action or procedure, nor be
served with process therein, nor have any knowledge thereof, nor in any case, unless the Company shall be actually prejudiced by
such failure.

Upon payment of any loss hereunder, the Company shall be entitled to be subrogated to all rights of insured against all other parties.

Upon a sale of the property covered hereby, this policy automatically thereupon shall become a warrantor's policy and the insured, his heirs, executors and administrators, shall for a period of twenty-five years from date hereof remain fully protected according
to the terms hereof by reason of the payment of any loss he or they may sustain on account of any warranty contained in the deed
executed by insured conveying said property. The Company to be liable under said.......

The original title. *Jim Williams.*

founder of Dickey's Barbecue Pit, telling her, "We're moving to a small
town called Preston Hollow" when she was eleven. Her parents, like many
of Preston Hollow's original residents, wanted acreage. Jim Williams said
that his family chose Preston Hollow because his mother fell in love with
a charming white home with a white fence she saw in the neighborhood

The Williams home in 1997. Like many other single-story ranch houses in the neighborhood, it has been demolished. *Jim Williams*.

when they moved from Greenville, Texas. Their home was built at 3835 Kenmore Drive (now 6402 Mimosa) in 1938. He remembers playing games with his friends and riding the Cotton Belt to go see his grandparents. Both he and his wife, Glenda, went to Preston Hollow Elementary and Hillcrest High School. During this four-year boom period, families would also move to Preston Hollow to start businesses and retail.

Sam Lobello Jr. purchased Tim McGraw's dairy farm at the southwest corner of Preston and Northwest Highway and opened a barbecue joint on July 2, 1938. He stated, "I take pleasure in announcing to the people my newest and only restaurant. It is the fulfillment of a dream which required approximately three years to come true. It is conveniently located on the Northwest Highway and Preston Road, across from the beautiful Preston Downs.* I dedicate the South's finest drive-in restaurant to those who enjoy good food served in a beautiful setting." Lobello's was the first business in Preston Hollow, and it served its residents for decades. The Lobello family sold the very corner to Magnolia Oil, which opened a gas station

---

* Preston Downs was the original name given to the area bordered by Preston, Northwest Highway, Deloache Avenue and the Cotton Belt tracks.

An opening-day advertisement for Lobello's. *Marguerite Archer.*

Above: Inside Lobello's.
Marguerite Archer.

Left: Sam Lobello Jr.
Marguerite Archer.

William Underwood's house at 5310 Park (1938).

in 1939. The building is now a Sleep Number mattress store. Also in the late 1930s, two men named William G. Underwood and Claude Ezell met with executives of Republic Pictures in Hollywood to discuss their ideas of bringing a new but quickly growing fad, the drive-in theater, to Dallas. The two men moved to Preston Hollow and purchased two neighboring lots: 5310 Park Lane and 9506 Meadowbrook Drive. They enlisted famous architect Charles Dilbeck to build both of their homes, which were completed in 1937–38. (Interior and exterior photos of both of these homes are featured in the last chapter.) Underwood and Ezell purchased the land at the northwest corner of Hillcrest and Northwest Highway and built a drive-in movie theater, the first in all of Dallas. It was named the Northwest Hi-Way Drive-In Theatre and opened on June 20, 1941. According to the *Dallas Morning News*, it "had a capacity for more than 450 vehicles"; additionally, "there were 204 loudspeakers on the property, one between every two cars." Tom Dunning remembers playing on the playground in front of the screen. Jim and Glenda Williams remember going on dates at the drive-in while they were attending Hillcrest High School. The Coffee Cup, a diner, later opened next door. Glenda said that it was "the place" for teens to go after school.

Above: The Northwest Hi-Way Drive-in Theatre. *Cinema Treasures.*

Left: The Coffee Cup, popular among teens, on Hillcrest. The top of the screen for the drive-in can be seen to the left of the water tower.

Even though Glen Lakes Country Club is outside the boundaries of Preston Hollow, many of its residents belonged to it. Founded in 1913 at the southwest and southeast corners of Walnut Hill and Coit (now Walnut Hill and US 75 Central Expressway), it was built as the Dallas Automobile Country Club, without a golf course. The name was changed to Glen Lakes Country Club in 1933, and a golf course was added. Twila Moore, who grew up on Lupton, said, "It was wonderful! We didn't have a pool and we could walk over and swim"; she also mentioned that her brother "could also walk over and fish in the pond." It closed in 1977, and the land was sold off for development. The area where the course was is now a gated community called Glen Lakes. The clubhouse, located east of Coit, was demolished, and apartments were built. Also located near Glen Lakes was an orphanage called the Reynolds Presbyterian Home. The kids

DALLAS AUTOMOBILE CLUB HOUSE, DALLAS, TEXAS
LANG & WITCHELL, ARCHITECTS   ::

The Glen Lakes Country Club clubhouse, built in the 1910s. *Flashback Dallas.*

attended Preston Hollow schools. Elizabeth Dickey Mills remembers them being the sweetest kids when she would have them over for soda parties. The orphanage was demolished in the early 1960s, and Texas Health Presbyterian Hospital Dallas was built in its place.

As more residents and businesses moved to Preston Hollow, the unorganized and unstructured way of running things was becoming obsolete. Like always, Ira DeLoache had a solution: Preston Hollow should become an incorporated township.

Chapter 3

INCORPORATED TOWNSHIP

1939–1944

*We really didn't know what we were doing, but you can't do better
than to be the first to start in a prime location of a growing city
and patiently build a magnificent church.*
—*Eric Ericson, one of the founders of Preston Hollow Presbyterian Church,
regarding the establishment of the church in Preston Hollow*

On November 18, 1939, a petition was signed by 230 residents urging Preston Hollow to become incorporated as a township. For an unknown reason, the official town boundaries included only what is today's "Old Preston Hollow." They went from "Northwest Highway to Park Lane, [and] Preston to Meadowbrook," leaving out all of the streets east of Preston. Following the election on December 20, 1939, the former mayor of Dallas, Joe Lawther, was elected as the mayor of Preston Hollow, William. H. Clark as city attorney and Herbert Otis as secretary. The members of the city council were Frank I. Brinegar, J.T. Martin, A.E. Hammerstein and G.L. Soelter. Ira DeLoache's real estate office on the northwest corner of Preston and Northwest Highway was turned into the town hall. Commonly referred to as a "do it yourself government," the Town of Preston Hollow was set up as a tax-free government, which meant that all of the city official positions, including police and fire departments, were volunteer. Residents were asked to contribute a twenty-five-dollar annual operating fee, which many refused to pay. The volunteer fire department was mainly staffed by sixteen- and seventeen-year-old boys,

Ticket for Preston Hollow

FRANK I. BRINEGAR.   A. E. HAMMERSTEIN.   G. L. SOELTER.

WILLIAM H. CLARK   J. T. MARTIN.   H. C. OTIS.

JOE E. LAWTHER.

Harmony ticket candidates for city officials of the newly incorporated town of Preston Hollow to be voted on Dec. 20 include the men pictured above.

Joe E. Lawther, Dallas Mayor during the World War, will be a candidate for Mayor of the new town. Candidates for Aldermen will be Frank I. Brinegar, A. E. Hammerstein, G. L. Soelter, William H. Clark Jr. and J. T. Martin. H. C. Otis is in the race for City Marshal. No opposing slate has been filed.

This 1939 newspaper article announced the candidates for Preston Hollow's government. All these men got elected. *Copyright 1939 The Dallas Morning News, Inc.*

Preston Hollow's former town hall at night.

as the eighteen-year-olds were fighting overseas in World War II, and a fire truck was purchased for them in 1943. The police officer, Leroy Trice, made his salary solely off of traffic fines he issued. His job was relatively peaceful, with the exception of a raid on a robber hideout at 6331 Meadow in the early 1940s. (This story is featured in Chapter 6.) A historical account written by an unknown person stated, "The town's single police officer spent most of his time directing traffic at the intersection of Preston and Northwest, where he wrote all those tickets to pay for his salary."

On February 25, 1940, the Town of Preston Hollow had its first major issue: alcohol. Of the people in the city limit who voted, 97 out of 146 voted to make the town "dry," meaning Preston Hollow could not sell alcohol. Ira DeLoache said that he was not opposed to Preston Hollow's residents consuming alcohol—he just didn't want people selling it in anywhere in Preston Hollow. The city officials drew a map and submitted it as a "dry zone" but left out a thirty-foot parcel of land. A clever entrepreneur purchased that land, near today's Preston Center, and opened a liquor store. Legend has it that this store was the only place to legally buy liquor from downtown Dallas to Missouri.

Joe E. Lawther decided to resign from office in April 1940, since there were not enough funds to run the township. On April 3, 1940, Mart W. Reeves was elected as the second mayor of Preston Hollow. Mart lived at 8530 Jourdan Way (1937), which was designed by famous architect Hal Thompson. This home still stands at the time of this writing. He left in place his predecessor's tax-free policy. As more businesses appeared in Preston Hollow, like the large drive-in theater, residents signed a petition against lights and loud music. They claimed that these businesses were disturbing their peace. An ordinance was passed in July 1940 regulating loud noises and bright lights.

Also in 1940, Kenneth Bouve, headmaster of the Texas Country Day School, wrote a report stating that if the school wanted a better reputation and greater success, it would need new facilitates: "Adequate quarters for the school are absolutely essential for the continuance of the school on the scale and with the standards required. Although we have no real competition in Texas, some people are not impressed by the simplicity of our set-up." The book *St. Mark's School of Texas: The First 100 Years* noted, "A converted garage and chicken coop fell short of what most parents expected from a good prep school"—students dubbed it "the shacks." President of the school board Wirt Davis told the school that he would fund the construction of a new building; however, he did not want this building to be constructed at the school's current campus at Preston and Walnut Hill. He persuaded Freeman Burford to purchase twenty-five acres three-fourths of a mile north of Walnut Hill for the building site (this plot of land is the current St. Mark's campus). Wirt Davis and the Texas Country Day School began construction on the new building in the spring of 1940, hoping to complete it for the 1940–41 school year. Preston Hollow resident Eugene McDermott (8626 Douglas, 1937), who was the president of what would become Texas Instruments, held a fundraiser that raised $3,700 for science equipment. McDermott was devoted to raising the quality of education in Dallas. The building, named Founders Hall in honor of the school's founding families, was completed at a cost of $75,000. The lease of Stichter's facilities and 6126 Lakehurst was terminated following the 1939–40 school year.

The school's 1942 catalogue described Founders Hall thusly:

> *The combined administration building and dormitory is of Williamsburg colonial design with modern construction throughout. The structure faces west on Preston Road, with class rooms in the center and north wing, and dining room and bedrooms in the south wing. The building has a large*

Texas Country Day School's new Founders Hall building, located at its current campus at 10600 Preston Road. *St. Mark's School of Texas.*

> *assembly room and study hall, ten class rooms, laboratories, the Hopkins Memorial Library, administration offices, dining room and kitchen facilities for one hundred-fifty persons, dormitory accommodations for thirty-five boarding students, an infirmary, two masters' suites, a Little Theatre in the garret, photographers' dark room, lounge and recreation room for the boarders....The McDermott Wood Working Shop, on the third floor, is completely equipped with power and hand tools and provides ample space and work benches for twelve boys at one time.*

In 1943, the school's football field, Bailey Field, was built. It was named after student Joseph W. Bailey III's father, who died in a car accident. His mother funded the entire field in memory of her husband. On the evening of November 13, 1943, while four faculty members were eating with twelve boarding students in the dining room, a student alerted the staff that he heard a crackling noise in the attic. When they rushed outside, they saw flames coming out of the roof near the center of the building. By the time the volunteer Preston Hollow Fire Department extinguished the fire five hours later, Founders Hall had only been reduced to its brick walls. Kenneth Bouve

The flag-raising ceremony. *St. Mark's School of Texas.*

struck a deal with Southern Methodist University president Umphrey Lee, who allowed the school to temporarily be housed in SMU classrooms as well as other offsite facilities until Founders Hall was rebuilt.

The relocation of the Texas Country Day School left vacant a parcel of very valuable land at a bustling intersection. With the 1940 census recording about 850 residents in just the Preston Hollow official city limits alone, there were probably, give or take, 2,500 residents in total, including those east of Preston. However, the exact number of residents is hard to calculate since many of the original homes have been torn down. In the early 1940s, many industries—like the Dallas Presbytery Extension Committee—took these growing numbers as a call to expand north. Hoping to plant a new church in Preston Hollow, the committee appointed Dr. Cecil H. Lang to command the project. Dr. Lang met with the pastor of Oak Cliff Presbyterian Church, Dr. Thomas Currie, and eight other people at Highland Park Presbyterian Church. Those eight people were Harry Crawford, Eric Ericson, Francel Ericson, Harry E. Blocker, Walter T. Weiderhold, Clifton Wilhite, Carmen Wilhite and C.J. Jenson. Eric Ericson served as the chairman of this committee, with Clifton Wilhite as the secretary. Dr. Lang hired David Pittenger, who was a seminary student at the time, to go door to door in Preston Hollow and ask the residents if they were interested in helping to establish a church. David claimed that he did not miss a single door!

When the first service was conducted by Dr. Lang, there were fifty-one attendees, all of whom were prospective members. Seventeen days after the initial service, Clifton Wilhite wrote and presented a petition, with sixty-seven signatures, to the Presbytery Office in Dallas, and it was quickly approved. An installation service was held electing elders, deacons and trustees, and on that same day, Reverend Robert "Manny" P. Douglass was called as the first pastor of Preston Hollow Presbyterian Church. Commenting on the founding of Preston Hollow Presbyterian Church, Eric Ericson stated, "We really didn't know what we were doing, but you can't do better than to be the first to start in a prime location of a growing city and patiently build a magnificent church." PHPC immediately began holding regular services at Texas Country Day School, but it presented challenges. Folding chairs and other church materials had to be carefully set up and then taken down every Sunday, which became more and more difficult as church attendance grew. Four months later, a building committee was established with W.C. (Dub) Miller and John Straiton as joint chairmen.

Reverend Robert P. Douglass.
Preston Hollow Presbyterian Church.

The first task was to decide the location. Originally, the congregation planned to build the church on a 3-acre lot at the corner of what is now Tibbs and Stichter Avenue, next to Preston Hollow Elementary School. However, a better option was available: the former Texas Country Day School campus. PHPC and Dub Miller decided to purchase this 6.2-acre plot at the southeast corner of Preston and Avalon (now Aberdeen). They hired architect Mark Lemmon, who designed a Georgian-style building with red brick and a slate roof, similar to that of SMU, Preston Hollow Elementary School and TCD's Founders Hall. Raising funds was a challenge. The presbytery donated $25,000, but this, in addition to member's donations of $35,505, was still not enough. PHPC was $25,000 short of qualifying for a loan, so many members committed the selfless act of mortgaging their homes, and Metropolitan Savings and Loan agreed to the $175,000 loan at 4.5 percent interest. The building plans were for a Georgian-style building consisting of a "Fellowship Hall seating 250 [to serve as a temporary sanctuary]; church school rooms; offices and a kitchen." A four-handled shovel was simultaneously used by Reverend Robert P. Douglass, Mrs. J.M. Smith, W.C. "Dub" Miller and John A. Straiton during the groundbreaking. While the building was under construction, services were moved to the auditorium of Preston Hollow Elementary School, which was more popular among the members since it featured built-in chairs.

Preston Hollow Presbyterian Church (PHPC) held its services at Texas Country Day School before its own building was completed. *Preston Hollow Presbyterian Church.*

The first service was held in the incomplete building on Thanksgiving Day and was described as a cold day with chattering teeth. The steel drums with charcoal fires burned, but they had little effect since there were no doors and windows. Elizabeth Dickey Mills, who lived at 9900 Preston, remembers seeing people attend that first service, saying, "It was Thanksgiving, and it was a very cold day. I had an unobstructed view of the door of Founders Hall. A tarp had been nailed to the top of the doorway and it was blowing wildly in the wind, and I could see people going in all bundled up." After dodging all of the financial obstacles and jumping all of the hurdles, the building was finally completed in 1952–53. The dedication day address was given by Dr. Robert F. Jones of First Presbyterian Church, Fort Worth. Dan Williams, Dr. Cecil Lang and Dr. John Anderson represented the presbytery. The Fellowship Hall, which sits on Aberdeen, was aptly named Founders Hall, in honor of the founders of the church. It still bears the same name today.

By the end of 1953, church membership had grown to 699 people. Howard Parker, who has been a member of PHPC since 1955, remembers being part of the Andrews Club. He, along with 11 other people, would

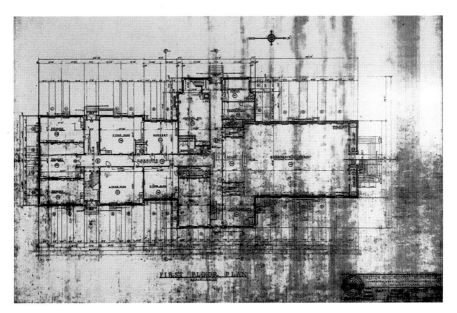

Mark Lemmon's architectural plans for PHPC. *Preston Hollow Presbyterian Church.*

The groundbreaking ceremony. *Preston Hollow Presbyterian Church.*

Above: Preston Hollow Presbyterian Church shortly after completion. *Preston Hollow Presbyterian Church.*

Right: Founders Hall shortly after completion. *Preston Hollow Presbyterian Church.*

have dinner in the church on Tuesday nights before venturing into the neighborhood to visit homeowners who wanted more information about joining the church. Over the next several years, the church would continue to make improvements, such as air conditioning throughout the entire facility and the addition of a gym to serve the youth. Barbara Pittenger, who served as PHPC's first youth director, remembers when the neighborhood children would roller-skate in the gym after school. In 1958, Ralph Stichter Jr., who had been a member of the church located just feet from his house,

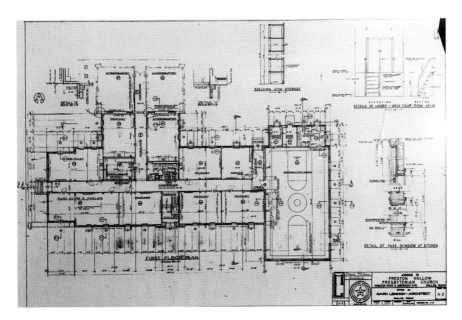

Above: Mark Lemmon's architectural plans for the 1958 addition. *Preston Hollow Presbyterian Church.*

Left: A worship service inside Founders Hall. *Preston Hollow Presbyterian Church.*

passed away. His wife, Mary Stichter, offered to sell the 3.5 acres to PHPC and moved to 6030 Woodland (1940). With the idea of constructing a larger sanctuary, the session immediately agreed to the purchase.

The passing of one of Preston Hollow's original settlers and the consequent demolition of his estate to make room for a new sanctuary for a growing church signified the continued desire for redevelopment in Preston Hollow. Without that important land acquisition, PHPC would not be the sizeable church it is today. At the time of purchase, the membership of Preston Hollow

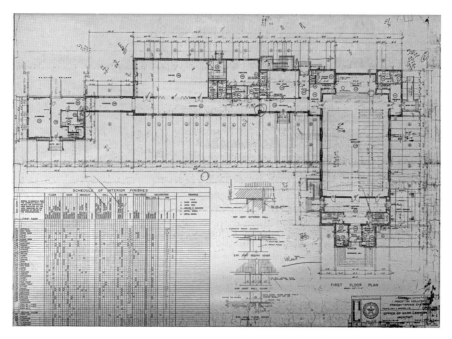

Above: The architectural plans for the sanctuary and the parlor. *Preston Hollow Presbyterian Church.*

Opposite, top: The exterior of PHPC's sanctuary.

Opposite, bottom: PHPC broke ground on its newest building, the Jubilee Expansion Building, on May 27, 2001. It was completed in 2002.

Presbyterian Church had grown to 1,478 parishioners, so the addition of a new space was a welcome one. According to the church, "the grounds were beautiful and there would be space for additional parking," adding that the purchase "was an opportunity for Preston Hollow to become a large, landmark church serving a much larger congregation." V.N. Burgess headed the building committee, and $721,400 was set aside for the approximate cost of construction. Stichter's house was demolished in 1961, and the church rehired architect Mark Lemmon, the same architect who designed the original building, to design the new sanctuary. He was instructed to closely match the architecture with that of the 1940s-style Georgian building, as opposed to building a Mid-century structure that many 1950s and 1960s churches featured. Today, Preston Hollow Presbyterian Church is one of the largest Presbyterian churches in the Dallas Fort Worth Metroplex.

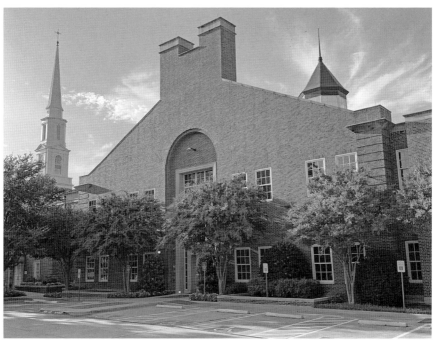

Because of domestic air raid threats occurring during World War II, the city council passed a "Blackout and Air Raid Protection" in January 1942. This instructed residents to comply with the army's and navy's recommendations stating that "in modern warfare no city, however distant from the enemy, is free from attack." Also in 1942, the city council imposed taxes for police and fire, since only one out of four residents paid the twenty-five-dollar protection fee. However, with the growing population, the do-it-yourself tax-free government was failing. Residents were tired of septic tanks and gravel roads, so they wrote a petition to the City of Dallas for annexation. On March 2, 1945, Mart Reeves passed an ordinance stating that he could hold an election regarding annexation.

Chapter 4

ANNEXATION AND AFTER

1945–1979

We are very proud of our new part of Dallas. We are going to do everything possible to make it one of the finest residential districts in the country. Its topography is beautiful and with the extension of municipal services which are not available now, we know Preston Hollow will be proud to be known as part of our city.
—*Dallas mayor Woodall Rodgers regarding the annexation of the city of Preston Hollow in April 1945*

S .J. Hay was the chair of a civic committee that created an analysis for the residents about joining Dallas. Included in this analysis was information about taxes, improved police and fire protection, a sewage system, service costs, garbage collection and other municipal issues. He and his committee were pro-annexation. He stated to the residents, hoping to persuade them to vote in favor of the annexation, "Frankly, we have found that our community is offered a great bargain. We can receive many benefits by uniting with Dallas." On April 3, 1945, an election was held for the residents in the city limits regarding annexation. The results were dramatically pro-annexation, with three hundred for and seventy against. On April 4, 1945, the mayor of Dallas, Woodall Rodgers, announced that Preston Hollow would become part of the city of Dallas. The areas that were annexed on that monumental day were today's Old Preston Hollow (bordered by Preston, Northwest Highway, Inwood and Walnut Hill); the streets of Northwood, Deloache, Woodland, Park and Desco in Preston Hollow East; Stichter's estate at Preston and Walnut Hill; and the area between Walnut Hill, Preston, the Cotton Belt and

DALLAS, TEXAS, THURSDAY, APRIL 5, 1945

—News Staff Photo.

PRESTON HOLLOW PARADE—Mayor Woodall Rodgers, in the driver's seat, and oth
ncilmen and city officials piled on the firetruck Wednesday preparatory to visiting Pre
ton Hollow and welcoming that area into Dallas.

A *Dallas Morning News* article regarding the "Preston Hollow Parade." *Copyright 1945 The Dallas Morning News, Inc.*

Dexter (today's Colhurst Avenue, not the present-day Dexter Drive), as well as even the northeastern part of Bluffview. Shortly thereafter, the remainder of Preston Hollow was annexed. Mayor Rodgers stated, "We are very proud of our new part of Dallas. We are going to do everything possible to make it one of the finest residential districts in the country. Its topography is beautiful and with the extension of municipal services which are not available now, we know Preston Hollow will be proud to be known as part of our city." He added that no commercial development would invade residential areas. He, as well as other Dallas city officials, filled a bus that displayed a banner that read "Preston Hollow, Here We Come." A parade, led by Dallas fire chief L.M. Funk, consisted of the bus, a police car, a shiny new fire truck, a garbage truck and, lastly, a truck containing sewer pipes. This parade, which journeyed through the streets of Preston Hollow, showed the residents the results of what they had voted for. According to Tom McCormack, Mayor Woodall promised the residents of Preston Hollow:

1. Services of the Dallas Police Department and Dallas Fire Department, with the existing police and fire units absorbed into the city of Dallas.
2. Garbage removal twice weekly without charge to the residents.
3. Street maintenance.
4. Water bills reduced to Dallas level and elimination of sewer charges.
5. No change in school tax assessments in the change from Vickery Independent School District to DISD.

6. Tax assessment to establish new values for Preston Hollow based on the Dallas tax rate of $1.54 per $100 valuation beginning in January 1946. Since the area has never established a complete taxing system and had only set aside a small portion for police and firefighting, a new system had to be developed. The large estates were handled on a combination of home and undeveloped property basis to prevent undue hardship.
7. Plans for a sanitary sewerage line and system to be put into effect as soon as "war conditions" permitted.
8. Establishment of better bus service to the area.
9. Establishment of a neighborhood zoning council.
10. Site for a new fire station.
11. No change in the Dallas City Council under the unification, since any increase would have been based on the possibility of the additional annexation of Highland and University Park.

During the last official city council meeting at Mart Reeves's house at 8530 Jourdan Way (1937), Preston Hollow's city council terminated Preston Hollow as a city and handed over the records in late April 1945.

Another thing that changed were the addresses and some street names. Prior to annexation, the street addresses in Preston Hollow were in the 3000s and 4000s, similar to University Park. In 1945, the addresses were changed to Dallas's 5000s and 6000s system, as they remain today. Avalon was renamed Aberdeen, Kenmore was renamed Mimosa, Armstrong was renamed Douglas, Dexter was renamed Colhurst (not to be confused with today's Dexter Drive) and Jordan Way was respelled Jourdan Way so it would not be confused with other Dallas streets.

The City of Dallas immediately began construction of new infrastructure in Preston Hollow. Work began on Preston Hollow Elementary School immediately after annexation, and the hope was for it to be ready for the 1945–1946 school year. However, it was not completed in time. Marietta Johnson, who was in first grade in 1945, remembers attending classes at Highland Park Presbyterian Church until the school building opened. Walnut Hill School and Hillcrest High School were annexed into the Dallas school system. Dallas also began construction on a new fire station at the southwest corner of Northwest Highway and Douglas. Dallas Fire Station No. 27 was completed in 1947 and demolished in about 2012 to make way for the current structure. At the time of construction, Station No. 27 served residents from Northwest Highway all the way north to the Collin County line. Preston Hollow Park—located at Thackery, Park Lane, Turtle Creek and Chevy Chase—was officially designated a City of Dallas park that same year.* A community pool, which is now just a concrete slab next to the tennis courts, was constructed near Turtle Creek and Park.

Dallas also made many road improvements. Before annexation, many the roads were gravel. The city would simply pave over all the gravel roads, but it told residents that if they wanted curbs and/or sidewalks, they would have to pay for those on their own. The residents of most blocks voted no to either of these things; however, many voted for just curbs. Few streets in Preston Hollow feature sidewalks, as most blocks found these an unnecessary purchase. This is why today it is inconsistent why some streets have a curb and/or a sidewalk while others don't. Preston, Northwest Highway and Walnut Hill were widened from country roads to three-by-three roads. Barbara Fix, who lived at the southeast corner of Inwood and Walnut Hill, remembers her father, George Fix, protesting the widening since it would eat up much of his property. In addition to city infrastructure, the remaining lots were built on after World War II, and these new homes featured state-of-the-art technology like cooling towers and dishwashers. Elizabeth Dickey Mills remembers going to see "The Parade of Homes" on Lupton in 1952. "When I was a teenager, I went reluctantly with my mother, she wanted to see them. She was totally dazzled, and even I was impressed. It was in the summer, and the houses were very very cool, almost chilly." Lupton was one the last streets developed in Preston Hollow, opening in the mid-1940s.

While the 1930s and early 1940s were the main periods of residential development in Preston Hollow, the 1950s would be the primary period for commercial development in the area. The first major business that moved into Preston Hollow was Neiman-Marcus. The luxury department store announced in January 1949 that it would be opening a sixty-three-thousand-square-foot store in Preston Center that would be designed by DeWitt & Swank. *Dallas Magazine* stated in February 1949 that the "new suburban shop of Neiman-Marcus Company is scheduled for construction this year in [Preston Center] on a plot 30,000 square feet facing Preston Road and extending from Wentwood to Villanova Drives," adding that "the store will… represent a total investment of about $1,500,000." The store was completed in 1951 and offered sophisticated fashion and lifestyle retail to local families.

---

* A sign at the corner of Thackery and Park Lane incorrectly states that the park was designated in 1949.

Apartments at the corner of Del Norte and Hillcrest in 1947. The rear of the Northwest Highway Drive-In Theatre is on the left side of the photograph. The land to the east of Hillcrest is Caruth family land that would become the site of Temple Emanu-El in the 1950s. *From the collections of the Dallas History & Archives Division, Dallas Public Library.*

Deloache Avenue (*bottom*) and Woodland Drive (*top*) in 1947. Note how all the houses on Woodland are small one-story ranch-style homes. *From the collections of the Dallas History & Archives Division, Dallas Public Library.*

The basement featured a toy department with a large mural of a forest and a giant cage that allegedly had an endless supply of stuffed animals. The store took on a southwestern tone and was furnished by interior designer Eleanor Le Maire, who featured many glass mosaics. Twila Moore remembers what she describes as "the beautiful Neiman's with the pretty windows." The store also featured a salon and restaurant.

The opening day, which was in October 1951, was a smashing success and drew large crowds. A statement from Neiman's from October 1951 noted:

> *Our new store at Preston Center is eight days old, and an eventful and hectic eight days they've been. If you should stumble over any prone bodies in the streets these days, the chances are they're just Neiman-Marcus merchandise managers, overcome with the strain....Opening day was very confusing. Even though we didn't announce the opening, simply to avoid the crowds that sort of announcement always brings, still a crowd showed up. The news spread fast by word of mouth that the new Neiman-Marcus store was open, and, by lunch time, the place was mobbed. So, if the service in the Kachina Room [its restaurant] was slow and it took you a long time to get luncheon, please forgive us and give us another try. The staff was just overwhelmed, and, now that they've got their feet back under them, we think you'll find our restaurant one of the best in town.*

The Neiman-Marcus executives added, "And, almost more than anything else, we think you'll enjoy the relaxed, informal atmosphere of Neiman-Marcus Preston Center. We think you'll find it's one of the pleasantest places in town in which to wander around and enjoy yourself." In 1960, the store headed a relief and supply drive that sent food and clothing to Chile, which had experienced many natural disasters simultaneously. The store closed in July 1965 when it relocated to NorthPark Mall. The building now houses multiple tenants, including Tootsies and Orvis.

Neiman-Marcus was not the only major department store chain to establish a store in Preston Center. Sanger's, later Sanger-Harris, opened its store in Preston Center in 1957. It was 242,000 square feet, much larger than Neiman-Marcus. The Preston Center store was its fourth store opened, following downtown Dallas, Highland Park Village and Oak Cliff Harris Center. The Sanger family lived at 5923 Averill Way (1933), which still stands. The store completed a major renovation in 1962 that featured higher-end sections and a parking garage. In a news feature from September 1962, an employee commented regarding the 1962 renovation:

Neiman-Marcus Preston Center in 1951. *The Department Store Museum.*

> *Many more customers are using our parking garage that adjoins the store, in which you can enter the store from each floor of the garage, even from the roof, and [a] very interestingly designed stairway comes down from the roof. Our new Carnation restaurant is so colorful and exciting….It's unique too and…it has the booths and individual seating arrangements. Many of our customers have told us they're very pleased that we now have the designer circle for our better fashions and our new apparel avenue in the Preston Center store. Our china, glassware, and gift shops in the decorative floor in the lower level is very interesting to shop through and browse. New taste and quality level at our store has taken on as we've done an interior rise, we particularly are pleased about our avenue of fashion, we think it is very pretty.*

The store became a Foley's in the 1990s when the two companies merged, and the store closed shortly thereafter when Foley's built its new store at NorthPark Mall. The building is now shared by Target, Marshalls, Gold's Gym, DSW, CVS and other smaller businesses.

As Preston Center became fully developed in the 1950s, demand brought the development of new retail even farther north. Construction began on the northeast corner of the Preston Royal Shopping Center in the mid-1950s. At this time, very little existed north of Royal Lane, Preston Hollow's present-day northern boundary, other than a few houses, a 7-Eleven and breakfast place at the northeast corner. The opening-day ceremonies for the new corner featured carnival rides in the parking lot and a ribbon cutting ceremony by Mayor Robert Lee Thornton. A state-of-the-art movie theater, the Preston Royal Theatre, opened at the northwest corner on November 11, 1959. Designed by architect Harold Berry, this theater featured many new forms of movie technology, like a wide screen and Victoria X projection. The theater had one thousand tangerine-colored seats, an aquarium and a garden, designed by architect Raymond F. Smith. Smith also designed another building across the street, Fire Station No. 41. The station opened on January 16, 1958. Unfortunately, it was completely destroyed in the October 20, 2019 tornado.

Kenneth Bouve, headmaster of Texas Country Day School, retired in 1949 and was replaced by Robert Iglehart. The Texas Country Day School, as well as the Cathedral School for Boys in downtown Dallas, were beginning to decline in popularity after the war since better public

The Preston Royal Theatre. *Cinema Treasures.*

schools, like Preston Hollow Elementary School, were now available to residents. The Cathedral School was established in 1946 when two schools, the Terrell School and St. Luke's, a school in Austin, merged. In 1949, many business leaders in Dallas, as well as Iglehart, pushed for TCD and Cathedral School to merge and form a superpower. The merger took place in September 1950 and formed what *TIME* magazine called the "best equipped day school in the country" in 1960, what is known today as St. Mark's School of Texas. Marietta Johnson, who works for St. Mark's, remembers how her childhood neighbor, Jack Foxworth, who lived on Deloache, kept a lion in his backyard for the mascot.

Another private school, this time an all-girls school, made its home in Preston Hollow. Ursuline Academy purchased 4838 Walnut Hill (1926) and relocated the school from its building on Bryan Street, renaming it Merici High School. The high school remained in this home until 1950, when it completed the construction of its current campus. Following the departure of Ursuline, a new school established its roots in Preston Hollow: Cistercian Preparatory School. Forty-seven boys arrived at 4838 Walnut Hill for their first day of school on September 5, 1962. Cistercian remained in this home until 1965. (The current address for 4838 Walnut Hill is 9950 Strait Lane.)

In 1957, Temple Emanu-El moved from South Boulevard to the northeast corner of Hillcrest and Northwest Highway, which was former Caruth family land. Founded as the first Jewish congregation in North Texas in 1875, today it is the largest Jewish congregation in the southern United States. Its current building, built in 1957, was designed by architects Howard R. Meyer, William W. Wurster and Max M. Sandfield. The architects received the Twenty-Five Year Award of Merit for their work in the building. Temple Emanu-El redesigned and expanded its campus in 2016 at a cost of $37 million.

At the time of annexation, the St. Louis Southwestern Railway (Cotton Belt) operated two passenger train services through Preston Hollow: the Lone Star, which ran from Memphis to Dallas, and the Morning Star, which ran from St. Louis to Dallas. Train stations serving Preston

Merici High School's senior classroom inside 4838 Walnut Hill (1926). *Lael Brodsky.*

Hollow were located at Meaders, which burned down in the mid-1940s, and Lovers Lane. Richard Scurry remembers hearing the trains whistle at the Park Lane and Walnut Hill crossings, as well as an overpass at NW Highway, rather than a traditional railroad crossing. He said that the trains rolling through shook and rumbled the whole neighborhood. Jim Williams remembers riding the train to see his grandparents. As the United States entered the automobile age, there was less demand for railroad service and more demand for roadways. The Cotton Belt ended both the Lone Star and Morning Star services in the early 1950s and replaced these services with a limited commuter service that connected passengers to other Cotton Belt services in northeast Texas. Cotton Belt passenger service to Dallas was ultimately discontinued by 1960. On June 9, 1953, the Texas Turnpike Authority was created by the Texas legislature. Bonds were issued in 1955 by the Texas Turnpike Authority for a proposed highway leading north from downtown Dallas, costing $33,650,000. Construction began on the Dallas North Tollway in 1966, and this initial stretch, which ran from Interstate 35E to Royal Lane, opened in 1968. The original plan was for the Tollway to become a

Left: Before: The Cotton Belt stop that was located at Lovers Lane.

Right: After: Construction crews built a bridge for the Dallas North Tollway at Lovers Lane where the Cotton Belt station used to exist. *From texasfreeway.com.*

free state highway once all debt was paid off. Jack Davis of the Texas Turnpike Authority noted, "When revenue bonds for a project are finally paid off…the facility reverts to the state as part of its highway system, to be used free."

Little changed in Preston Hollow during the 1960s and 1970s. Existing homeowners proudly maintained their homes, while new homeowners continued to move into the highly sought-after neighborhood.

Chapter 5

REDEVELOPMENT

1980–Present

My philosophy has always been about trying to really thoughtfully understand
what's currently happening and then thoughtfully plan.
—*Jennifer Staubach Gates, Dallas city councilwoman representing Preston*
Hollow from 2013 to 2021, regarding redevelopment in Preston Hollow

During the 1970s, Preston Hollow was beginning to lose popularity. All the attention was on fresh and new developments north of LBJ and even the suburbs of Plano and Frisco. Businesses, one by one, left Preston Center for NorthPark Mall. Glenda Williams said, "The biggest loss to the center was when Neiman-Marcus moved from the east side to NorthPark in 1965." She remembers it being "a huge loss, and [it] created a domino effect of others following their lead." Pretty much no new development occurred because everything had been built up thirty to forty years earlier, but the demand for redevelopment was nonexistent. Thankfully, famous realtors, like Ebby Halliday, continued to keep the neighborhood housing flow going.

Beginning her career by selling hats in 1938, Ebby entered the real estate market by making "decisions based on emotions rather than rational thought." She was known for staging her houses with detail and personal touches. She would always say, "Our job is to give them a better idea what the house will look like after they move in." Today, Ebby Halliday is one of the largest real estate companies in all of Texas. In 1964, hoping to better serve the Preston Hollow area, it purchased DeLoache's former office/ Preston Hollow Town Hall for $100,000 and paid $50,000 for repairs. Ebby told the *Dallas Morning News* in 2012, "Getting that building was a dream come true for me....Who wouldn't want this?" Mary Frances Burleson told the *Dallas Morning News* that the building was cheaply built and not meant to last decades. She also said that the building caught fire in the 1970s! Halliday built her residence behind the office in 1967, and it still stands today. The Ira DeLoache office and Halliday's residence were both nominated for a City of Dallas Historic Designation in 2019.

The Mayflower Estates neighborhood, which was mainly developed in the 1960s and 1970s by Sam Lobello Jr., is bordered by Walnut Hill, Inwood, Royal and the Tollway. It was developed on the land that was the Lobello family's estate. Their house was located at 5414 Ursula (1949). Lobello partnered with architect Charles Dilbeck, who designed many of the houses. While some say it is a subdivision of Preston Hollow, others claim that Mayflower Estates is its own neighborhood apart from Preston Hollow. Regardless, Mayflower Estates is home to many prime examples of Mid-century modern homes, as well as some of the most monumental multi-acre estates in all of Dallas. The famous Pio Crespi estate is located in Mayflower Estates.

The mid- to late 1980s, however, were a big growth period for Dallas. Many people relocated to Dallas toward the end of the twentieth century, and they were looking for something different. These people wanted to live in an old neighborhood with large trees and a community feel, but most importantly, they wanted to be close to downtown Dallas. They didn't want the suburbs, but they wanted houses like the new ones built in the suburbs with five to six thousand square feet and high ceilings. Preston Hollow's prewar houses, many of which were single-story homes around two to three thousand square feet, could not fit these modern demands. Ultimately, beginning in the mid-1980s, one by one, old homes were demolished and replaced with houses twice their size, in the estate area all the way to the one-third-acre lots east of Preston. "Property values are increasing at record rates," said Chris Dauwe, co-owner of Rosewood Custom Home Builders, adding that Preston Hollow is "just a nice place to raise a family—there's nothing really negative besides the heat."

Chris Dauwe's father, Luc Dauwe, first started building new homes in Preston Hollow in 1994. Rosewood, along with other successful home building companies in Preston Hollow, are more attentive to personal preference and design than ever. Chris said, "People are not really considering their homes as just a home anymore—it's a showpiece." In the 1990s, the styles of new homes being built in Preston Hollow were all very similar. People would see other homes in the neighborhood and want

Some original homes, like this house at 6303 Lakehurst (1936), have been renovated to meet today's standards, while others have been torn down to make way for new development. *Full Package Media.*

Inside the updated 6303 Lakehurst (1936). *Full Package Media.*

Above: One of Rosewood's new Preston Hollow Homes, at 6631 Stefani (2020).

Left: Chris and his father, Luc Dauwe, of Rosewood have built many new homes in Preston Hollow since the '90s. *Chris Dauwe.*

the same exact style. But in more recent years, Preston Hollow has turned into a showcase of architectural styles from around the world, featuring custom, one-of-a-kind homes. Scott Faulkner, CEO of Faulkner Perrin Custom Homes, a major builder in Preston Hollow, said that Preston Hollow "is simply just too beautiful [of] a place to have 'cookie cutter' homes built" and that "[being] mindful of the incoming residents' desires focusing on unique architecture and interior design combinations [will] add to the already rich history of the Preston Hollow neighborhood." He

Scott Faulkner (*left*) and Kirk Perrin (*right*) of Faulkner Perrin Custom Homes. *Scott Faulkner.*

feels that "it is a privilege to be a part of the community, not only as a builder but also as a company that has the opportunity to be instrumental in the creation of the future history of Preston Hollow." He hopes that the new homes will "be a blessing to the current residents by designing and constructing homes that they would approve of."

Preston Hollow today features many prime examples of antebellum (Greek Revival/Georgian), Shaker, Italianate, Shingle/Classical Revival, Tudor, bungalow, rambler/traditional brick, Colonial Revival, Mediterranean, Tuscan villa, French country, Contemporary, Mountain Modern and the newest trend, Texas Modern (contemporary farmhouse). Chris Dauwe of Rosewood thinks that the largest influence on the architectural designs is the internet and social media pages. "Those types of websites and social media venues are easy to flip through with your phone at night, so you can create a portfolio of your design rather quickly, and it's from around the world." He thinks that another factor is the number of people moving to the neighborhood from outside Texas: "A lot of influence [is] coming from where those people are moving from....They're bringing a lot of cool, trendy ideas."

In addition to the redevelopment of homes, Preston Hollow has seen its fair share of commercial and high-rise development in recent years, most notably near Preston and Northwest Highway. The first major commercial redevelopment was in the spring of 1995, when developers planned to demolish about 150 apartments at the corner of Turtle Creek and Northwest Highway that were built on the land of the former Northwest Hi-Way Drive-In Theatre, which closed in the early 1960s.

6542 Northwood (2005) is of French country design.

The large home at 6311 Northport Drive, built in 2006.

A Mediterranean-style home at 6307 Woodland (2003).

This Tuscan-style home is located at 6330 Park Lane (2006).

6347 Woodland, built in 1996.

The plan was to build a shopping center with a Tom Thumb grocery store, but this was quickly protested by neighbors. Fast-forward twenty years and the most controversial redevelopment project to date was about to begin.

Transwestern, a commercial real estate company from Houston, released plans in December 2013 to demolish an apartment complex at the northeast corner of Preston and Northwest Highway and the townhouses on Townhouse Row, which used to branch off from Averill Way, a street named after Ira DeLoache's son. The specs of the plans consisted of 296 two- and three-bedroom units in an eight-story building. On January 25, 2014, neighbors converged at the Black Eyed Pea restaurant, which used to stand in Preston Center, and met (and argued with) Mark Culwell, who was a senior vice-president at Transwestern. A petition was created against the high-rise development that gained more than one thousand signatures. Many neighbors also planted "No 8-Story High Rise" signs in their front yards. On February 21, 2014, residents packed into Preston Hollow Park for a rally against Transwestern and its plans. Afterward, the company declared that it would only build six stories rather than the original eight. It later downsized its plans from six to four stories, with only 196 units. Eventually, The Laurel was completed as only a four-story building (half as tall as originally planned), stair-stepping its way down as it gets closer to Del Norte. It was a fair tradeoff between what the residents and Transwestern wanted.

"My philosophy has always been about trying to really thoughtfully understand what's currently happening and then thoughtfully plan," said Dallas city councilwoman Jennifer Staubach Gates, who represented Preston Hollow from 2013 to 2021. At the turn of the decade, she had been working closely on studies about PD15, which would potentially replace a three-story condo complex that burned down in 2017 with one as high as twenty-two stories. Just like the Laurel project, many residents, especially those closest to Northwest Highway, are against the project. The biggest reason people are skeptical is the impact this would have on traffic. However, Councilwoman Gates conducted a study that proved, "If you have more of the amenities related to work, live, play, you can cut down on traffic," meaning if people can live, eat/shop and work near Preston Center, less daytime traffic would be present on Northwest Highway. Another controversial project Councilwoman Gates monitored was the proposal to demolish the two-story parking garage on the west side of Preston Center and replace it with an underground one twice the size with a park on top. Developers want to share the park space with a tall high-rise. However, residents are again skeptical about this proposal.

Despite all the progress that has been made, many people, especially those who have lived in the neighborhood for many years, oppose the redevelopment. They claim that the demolition of older homes is ruining the neighborhood and dub the new homes "starter castles" and "McMansions." In 2002, the National Trust for Historic Preservation described redevelopment as "an epidemic wiping out historic neighborhoods one house at a time." Preston Hollow has lost many monumental and significant homes over the years. DeLoache's homestead on Preston and countless Dilbecks are on that list. In the late 1980s, one builder purchased 6207 Glendora (1929) and tried to split it into two seventy-foot lots. Residents quickly protested this action, signing a petition against it. Jo Ann Parham remembers that some even went to court. The idea of the split lot was quickly blocked, and the house, one of the first built in Preston Hollow, survives today. This is not always the case, however, and many larger lots are indeed split into multiple units by developers. Barbara Fix recently lost her childhood home at 9910 Inwood (1946), which sits on a 5.22-acre lot, to developers hoping to build multiple houses on the tract of land. Some homeowners see this as gentrification that continues to keep

The former home of Ted and Twila Moore was one of the finest of its day upon its completion in 1935. This charming two-story home sat gracefully on its 0.73-acre lot, which is very uncommon for lots east of Preston. However, these days, the unusually large lot is more valuable to most. Unfortunately, it was demolished in 2019 and split into two lots. *Twila Moore.*

The iconic Preston Royal Shopping Center sign leaning against a damaged tree. *Wendy Hermes.*

our neighborhood on the map and extremely desirable almost one hundred years later. In many places the addition of the new homes has enhanced the splendor of the historic and original homes.

On Sunday, October 20, 2019, an EF-3 tornado touched down near State Highway 348 and Luna Road at 8:53 p.m. The tornado, with winds near 125 miles per hour, tore through the Marsh and Midway area along Walnut Hill. By the time the tornado reached Preston Hollow at about 9:05 p.m., winds near 140 miles per hour were being reported. After crossing the Dallas North Tollway, the tornado passed through the Preston Royal Shopping Center. It caused significant damage to all four corners of the complex, completely destroying Fire Station No. 41 and the southeast retail corner; every store in the main strip was demolished except for Central Market.

Bricks, tree limbs and other debris pile the parking lot of Preston Royal Shopping Center. *Wendy Hermes.*

Talbots' roof completely collapsed. *Wendy Hermes.*

Cloths lie piled in the center of this store following its windows being blown out. *Wendy Hermes.*

A photo taken by the author while flying a plane one day after the tornado showing the damage of St. Mark's and the surrounding houses. Note the vehicles thrown into the tennis courts.

A car damaged by the tornado. The house in the background is missing a good portion of its roof. *Sarah Are.*

An upturned car thrown next to a house. *Sarah Are.*

In Preston Hollow, the tornado damaged countless homes on Brookshire, Northport, Pemberton, Orchid, Tulip and Camellia Streets, as well as St. Mark's. The strongest point of the whole tornado was reported near Tibbs at 9:07 p.m.

In addition to Preston Hollow, damage in between the Tollway and US 75 Central Expressway occurred in the neighborhood north of Royal Lane (most notably wind damage to Lavendale and Azalea), as well as the Brookshire Park neighborhood southeast of Hillcrest and the Hillcrest Forest neighborhood. This tornado was the costliest tornado in all of Texas history, with property damage totaling $1.55 billion. Miraculously, there were zero human casualties, and only fifteen people were taken to local hospitals. Many credit this to the fact that the Dallas Cowboys football game was on and people were awake watching it. On Monday morning, Preston Hollow Presbyterian Church immediately jumped into action by serving breakfast and coffee to the homeowner victims of the tornado and the multitude of workers who had descended on the neighborhoods to help them. The church quickly initiated a relief plan, using its "Holy Roller" golf carts (usually used to transport people from the far end of the parking lot to the church building) to transport food and other supplies. Food donations quickly poured in from the congregation as well as many other sources. By Tuesday morning, Highland Park Presbyterian Church,

Golf carts, many of which were temporarily donated to PHPC for tornado relief, lined up behind the Youth House and being loaded before bringing food and other supplies into the neighborhood. *Sarah Are.*

Many houses, like Royce and Aimee Ramey's home on Pemberton (2019), had to be demolished due to substantial tornado damage. *Aimee Williams-Ramey.*

Highland Park Methodist Church and the Harwood family had lent their golf carts and street-legal mules to PHPC, and many members and staff from their congregations were taking part in relief efforts, supplying food to not only those affected by the tornado but also the workers and Dallas police officers protecting the neighborhood. Temple Emanu-El and Good Shepherd Episcopal also participated in PHPC's relief efforts. On Friday, October 25, 2019, Mi Cocina hosted a community lunch at Preston Hollow Presbyterian Church. In all, Preston Hollow Presbyterian Church delivered more than five thousand meals using eleven golf carts manned by more than one hundred volunteers during that first week. Countless school supplies were donated to Walnut Hill Elementary School, Edward H. Cary Middle School and Thomas Jefferson High School, all of whose buildings were severely damaged. Numerous homes were also heavily damaged, many of which had to be demolished and completely rebuilt.

Preston Hollow will continue to be Dallas's prime neighborhood, with its beautiful trees, streets and community feel. More original homes will be lost forever, and more new ones will be built. But the history will be remembered forever, and new stories will be added to it.

Chapter 6

SIGNIFICANT HOMES

It's easy to recognize a Dilbeck house. You don't have to put a sign out or look up the information of who the architect was—they're so distinctive.
—Thomas C. May, owner of the 1935 Charles Dilbeck–designed house at 5252 Ravine since the 1970s

Despite demolitions, many historic and architecturally significant homes remain in Preston Hollow. Eight homes built during the 1920s still stand in Preston Hollow, all of which are featured in this chapter. Architect Charles Dilbeck designed many homes in Preston Hollow, thirteen of which still stand. Many of those are also featured in this chapter, complete with their history and photos. All of the current owners of the Dilbeck homes were given the opportunity to have their home featured in this book.

1920s

6126 LAKEHURST

6126 Lakehurst was built by Ralph Benjamin Stichter in 1922 as a wedding gift for his son, Ralph Stichter Jr., and his new bride, Mary Stuart Stichter. This home is one of the oldest in Preston Hollow and one of the first two houses ever built in the neighborhood that was not associated with a farm (the other being Stichter's main house at Preston and Walnut Hill, now demolished, which was built about the same time). When Ralph Stichter

6126 LAKEHURST

6126 Lakehurst was built by Ralph Stichter Sr. in 1922 for his son as a wedding gift.

Sr. died in 1932, Ralph Stichter Jr., who lived in this house, moved to the main estate at Preston and Walnut Hill. When Stichter Jr. moved out, the home was leased to the Texas Country Day School (now St. Mark's), which allegedly held its very first classes there while Stichter's gatehouse off Preston Road near the main estate was being converted into a school building, making this house very likely the birthplace of the TCD. Donald Allen, who was one of the first teachers at TCD, stated, "I taught my first chemistry class of four students in a very tiny upstairs room in the garage." This possibly refers to the guest room still located above the garage, which was original to the property.

When the Texas Country Day School moved to Preston and Walnut Hill in September 1933, Kenneth Bouve, the headmaster and founder of Texas Country Day School, and his wife moved into the house. Beginning in 1935, the house was used as a dormitory for boarding students attending the school. The 1938 *Latigo* yearbook describes "a large, comfortable house…on Lakehurst Street, a few blocks away, [was] used as a dormitory and a residence for the Head Master. There were three boys in the dormitory the first year; two years later there were fifteen." The students got their water from a well in the backyard before city water reached Lakehurst Avenue. Many students boarded in this house throughout the 1930s and 1940s until a dorm was built on their new campus. The house was sold off by the Stichters, and its ties to Texas Country Day School and St. Mark's were lost. During the early 1950s, the western edge of the property was sold off, and a house, 6124 Lakehurst, was built. The house changed ownership many times throughout the '50s, '60s and '70s. Gladys (last name unknown), a neighbor across the street from 6126 Lakehurst, described the house in the 1960s and 1970s:

> *The red two story was built in 1922. A judge Randolph Caldwell and his young wife and two small boys lived there. The judge got it on money he was owed for his lawyer's work. He spent much money on it. The basement was always full of water. They didn't live there very long, maybe 10 years. It sold many times while we lived across the street, and all the people who bought it spent scads of money redoing the place. Everyone did something different to it.*

Actor Billy Crudup and his family lived in this house in the 1970s. In 1980, Michael and Jo Ann Parham bought the house, and she still lives there; sadly, Michael passed away in 2019. In an interview, Jo Ann described the house when they bought it as being in a state of disrepair, with the original plaster ceilings falling down, and there was an illegal interior fireplace. She said she paid a workman $200 to remove the original fireplace, and he described it as "the hardest work he had ever done." Old sinks were found in the upstairs bedrooms' closet. They were potentially used as half-bath sinks for the boarding kids to wash up and brush their teeth. The shims on floors in the family room had come loose, causing the floors to be unstable. A cracked tennis court was in the back, once an after-school activity for the boys, but it had to be removed. The Parhams put much time and money into the house to not only bring it up to date but also restore it to its original glory. In 1990, Jo Ann was asked by the production team of the movie *Bottle Rocket* if they could film a scene utilizing the tree in the front yard. They paid her $300 to film the front of the house and their tree. The scene, however, was not used in the movie. One hundred years later, the house still stands proud on the corner of Lakehurst and Tulane. Many pass by the house not knowing its importance and significance to the neighborhood. It is a true monument to the history of this neighborhood and St. Mark's. This home is currently in the process of receiving a designation by the Texas Historical Commission.

6126 LAKEHURST

Right: The garage and guest house.

Below: Inside the guest house.

6126 LAKEHURST

Top, left: A spiral staircase.
Top, right: A little window that overlooked the original front door, a feature common on early 1920s houses.
Bottom: Side view of 6126 Lakehurst.

6126 LAKEHURST

Above: The living room.

Left: Mike and Jo Ann Parham. *Jo Ann Parham.*

Top, left: The staircase.

Top, right: The chimney.

Bottom: The front of the house in 1980. *Jo Ann Parham.*

6126 LAKEHURST

Left: The tree used in *Bottle Rocket*.

Below: The house being renovated. *Jo Ann Parham.*

6126 LAKEHURST

Left: The family room.

Below: Workers in the family room. *Jo Ann Parham.*

6126 LAKEHURST

The original fireplace. *Jo Ann Parham.*

The new fireplace. *Jo Ann Parham.*

Left: The poorly added laundry room before it was rebuilt. *Jo Ann Parham.*

Right: An old bathroom that most likely looked this way during the dorm era before being renovated. *Jo Ann Parham.*

The new chimney being built.
Jo Ann Parham.

6331 MEADOW

This house was built in 1923 and lived in by a family until one of the parents was murdered in the early 1930s.* The family moved out, and the house sat vacant for many years—a home that had been the location of a murder was quite unappealing. A group of Preston Hollow robbers squatted in the house and vandalized it, breaking the windows and putting holes in the walls. In the mid-1940s, the Preston Hollow sheriff was planning to raid the house and capture the robbers. He positioned the person who lived in 6338 Meadow, which is catty-corner to 6331, in his upstairs window with a shotgun in case anything went wrong. After the robbers were captured, the vandalized house remained vacant. In the 1950s, the Lily family bought it for $2,000, almost next to nothing at that time. Even after they bought the house, it was still known as the "haunted house." They restored the home but sold it after a few years. The house changed hands two times until T.D. and Martha Dickey (who owned

*. The house was demolished in November 2020.

Dickey's Barbecue Pit) bought it in the mid-1960s. They asked their bank for a $50,000 loan to expand the house. They were denied this money because the bank told them that Preston Hollow was not a neighborhood prestigious enough for this kind of loan!

Opposite: 6331 Meadow.

Right: The front door.

6331 MEADOW

Above: The front windows.

Left: A bay window.

6331 MEADOW

Right: A little window overlooking the front door, similar to 6126 Lakehurst.

Below: The grand staircase.

6331 MEADOW

The top of the staircase.

The original fireplace.

9950 Strait (4838 Walnut Hill)

This historic house was built in 1926 on a twenty-seven-acre property just south of Walnut Hill and west of Inwood, with the address being 4838 Walnut Hill. It was built for the part owner of the A.A. Jackson & Brother produce company, Albert Allen Jackson. His father-in-law, C.C. Williams, designed the house. It features Neoclassical and Georgian Revival styles. Albert Jackson passed away in 1937 from a stroke, and the house was sold to Ursuline Academy on September 9, 1942. The academy relocated the school from its building on Bryan Street and renamed it Merici High School. The high school remained in this home until 1950, when it completed the construction of its current campus. The home, similar to 6126 Lakehurst, was converted into a dorm and used by Ursuline until the 1960s.

Following the departure of Ursuline, a new school was established in the home: Cistercian Preparatory School. On September 5, 1962, forty-seven boys arrived at 4838 Walnut Hill for their first day of school. Student Brian

9950 Strait.

9950 STRAIT (4838 WALNUT HILL)

Melton told his mother that first day, "If you think I'm going into that creepy old place, you're crazy." According to Cistercian's newspaper, *The Continuum*, regarding the home itself, "If the first-floor classroom felt elegant, its upstairs counterpart could safely be regarded as spectacular. Upon entering for the first time, the students were struck by the far, southern end of the room with its semi-circular shape and seven picture windows, which bathed the room in light and offered a view of the thick trees in back of the house." The home and its 9 acres (the rest had been absorbed by Ursuline for its own campus) were a hit among the students, who especially loved recess. Four square was played on the driveway, soccer and football on the front lawn and many other games throughout the woods and along Bachman Branch Creek. Marguerite Archer, daughter of Sam Lobello Jr., attended school in this house. She recalls feeling like she wasn't away from home at all. The final year Cistercian held classes in 4838 Walnut Hill was in 1965. In 1970, the estate was sold off and split into multiple lots, and the address was changed to 9950 Strait Lane. Today, the house sits on 1.1 acres. The house still contains many of its original features and is a relic of historic Preston Hollow and the schools that were once housed there.

9950 STRAIT (4838 WALNUT HILL)

Opposite: The library. *Lael Brodsky.*

Right: Albert Allen Jackson. *Lael Brodsky.*

Below: The back of the house.

9950 STRAIT (4838 WALNUT HILL)

Top: The senior classroom today. *Bottom*: The staircase.

9950 STRAIT (4838 WALNUT HILL)

Top: The fireplace today. *Bottom*: One of Cistercian's classrooms in the house. *Lael Brodsky.*

6303 MEADOW

6303 Meadow was built in 1927 as part of a dairy farm. Unfortunately, not much history is known about the farm.

6303 Meadow.

5111 PARK LANE

5111 Park Lane was built in 1928 for William T. and Susannah Harris. The house was originally brick, but it was stuccoed over. This is the oldest house in the neighborhood that is associated with the DeLoache/Joyce development.

Top: 5111 Park.

Bottom: The back of the Harris residence.

6207 GLENDORA

6207 Glendora was built in 1929 by architect Arthur E. Thomas for Polish-born Nathan Wohlfeld, who worked in the concrete industry. It features a prairie fire wall wrapping around the back side of the property. The west side of the house was added in the early 1950s. The Wohlfeld descendants lived in the house until 1980.

Opposite: 6207 Glendora.

Above: The side of the house.

Right: The stained-glass window.

6207 GLENDORA

Top: The pool and back of the house. *Bottom:* The living room with the stained-glass window.

Top: The dining room. *Bottom*: The house in the 1950s. *Todd and Shelly Groves.*

6207 GLENDORA

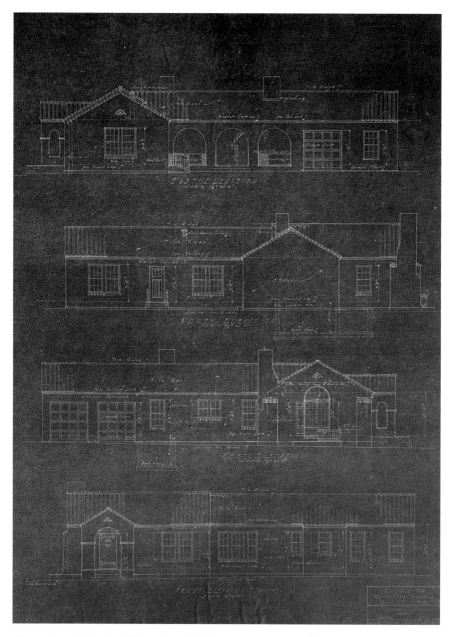

Above and opposite: Arthur Thomas's original architectural plans. *Todd and Shelly Groves.*

6207 GLENDORA

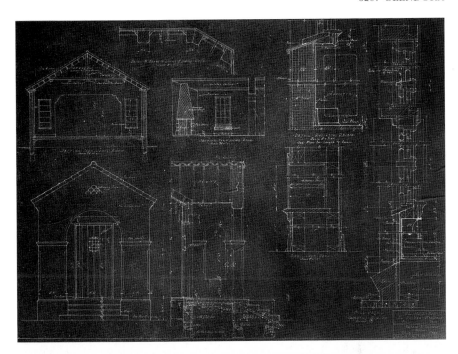

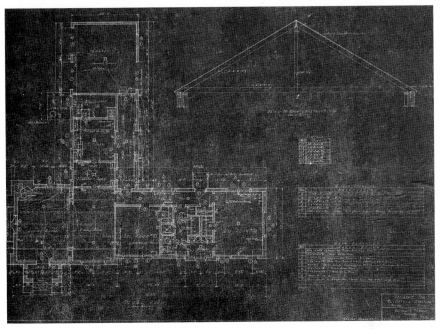

6207 GLENDORA

The original boiler in the basement.

9700 INWOOD

9700 was built in 1929 and was the first house on Inwood Road in Preston Hollow. When this house was built, Inwood in Preston Hollow only spanned from Park Lane to the front of this house. The original owners are unknown.

The living room.

9700 INWOOD

9700 INWOOD

Opposite, top: 9700 Inwood.

Opposite, bottom: The staircase.

Above: Interior.

Left: The original front entry.

9700 INWOOD

Opposite, top: The side.

Opposite, bottom: The back of the house.

Above: The back of the house in 1985. *Jeremy and Nancy Halbreich.*

Left: The original front entry in 1985. *Jeremy and Nancy Halbreich.*

5220 PARK

Built for the Walker E. Jackson family in 1929, this house was one of the first homes built on Park Lane. There were still cornfields in the backyard when this house was first built.

Above: 5520 Park.

Opposite, top: The back of the house.

Opposite, bottom: The living room.

Charles Dilbeck

5252 Ravine (1935)

Built in 1935 for Donald and Mary Anderson, this home features Chicago warehouse brick and the signature Dilbeck wood shingle roof that, due to age, has been removed on most other Dilbecks. The current owners, who have lived there since the 1970s, previously lived in a Dilbeck (now demolished) on Miron Drive. Thomas May remembers calling Charles Dilbeck himself to add another bedroom to their house on Miron. After not hearing from him for six months, he called Dilbeck again, who told him, "Don't rush an architect," and hung up the phone.

Above: 5252 Ravine.

Opposite: The back.

5252 RAVINE

5252 RAVINE

Opposite, top: The side.

Opposite, bottom: The garages.

Above: Chicago warehouse brick.

Right: The front door.

5252 RAVINE

The family room.

6315 LAKEHURST (1935)

6315 Lakehurst was built in 1935 and was the first house built on the block of Lakehurst from Tulane to Tibbs. Not much else is known about the history of the home. Additions were made on the eastern part of the home in the 1980s that did not match the Dilbeck style. When the current owners purchased the house in the 1990s, they hired a special architect to redo the addition, closely matching the Dilbeck style.

The front.

6315 LAKEHURST

Above: 6315 Lakehurst.

Left: A unique front window.

Above: Dilbeck's signature brick.

Right: The fence.

6315 LAKEHURST

Above: The back.

Left: The chimney.

The living room.

6315 LAKEHURST

Above: Dilbeck windows.

Left: Dilbeck doors.

9506 Meadowbrook (1937)

9506 Meadowbrook was built for Claude Ezell, who, with partner William Underwood, brought the drive-in movie business to Dallas, opening the Northwest Hi-Way Drive-In Theatre in Preston Hollow in June 1941. Dilbeck was commissioned to build his estate, and it was completed in 1937–38. His partner William Underwood's home was built by Dilbeck next door. An addition was made on the back side of the home in the 1990s that was also built in the Dilbeck style.

A screened-in porch.

9506 MEADOWBROOK

Above: Claude Ezell's house at 9506 Meadowbrook (1938).

Left: The staircase.

Above: The front.

Right: Dilbeck windows.

9506 MEADOWBROOK

Opposite: The back.

Above: The fireplace.

5310 PARK (1937)

Built in 1937 for William George Underwood, this home is the first Dilbeck in all of Dallas to receive a historical designation. Underwood and partner Claude Ezell established the drive-in theater at Hillcrest and Northwest Highway. The home was built with a pool house and a large screened-in porch. The garden was designed by famous landscape designer Joe Lambert Jr. He also designed the gardens of the Beverly Hilton Hotel, the TresVidas Golf Club and even the Texas Governor's Mansion. The garden features a pecan tree, two Bois D'Arc trees, two cedar elm trees and two magnolia trees. The current and third owner, who has lived in the home since 1970, with the help of Nancy McCoy, received a designation from the Dallas Landmark Commission that would preserve the home and garden's original character. Dilbeck, commenting on this house, said, "A house I did for W.G. Underwood is not really a Ranch house and yet it is a very interesting Ranch house. It has a handmade tile roof on it—very beautiful—different from anything in Dallas."

Above: 5310 Park Lane.

Opposite, top: The signature Dilbeck entry gate.

Opposite, bottom: The pool house.

5310 PARK

Top: A balcony. *Bottom*: A screened-in porch.

Top: The fireplace. *Bottom*: The beams.

9239 HATHAWAY (1937)
This home was built in 1937. Charles Dilbeck himself revisited the house in the late 1980s while it was being modernized.

Above: 9239 Hathaway.

Opposite, top: The side.

Opposite, bottom: The backside of the garages.

9239 HATHAWAY

9239 HATHAWAY

Above: The garages.

Left: The summer house.

Above: The fireplace.

Right: A Dilbeck column.

6122 DELOACHE (1938)

This home was built in 1938 for Malcolm Cloyd. He also purchased the lot to the east, 6132 Deloache. He rehired Dilbeck in 1951 to build a home on the eastern lot for his mother-in-law. This home has been the site of many Dilbeck home tours hosted by Preservation Dallas.

Above: The back.

Opposite, top: 6122 Deloache.

Opposite, bottom: The front door.

6122 DELOACHE

6122 DELOACHE

Above: The backside of the house.

Left: The back door and fireplace.

The staircase. *Linda Wilson.*

6122 DELOACHE

A fireplace.

The main fireplace.

6027 GLENDORA (1938)

Built in 1938, very little survives about the original history of this home. This house is similar in style to many of Dilbeck's Tulsa homes.

Above: 6027 Glendora.

Left: The front door.

6027 GLENDORA

Above: Dilbeck brick.

Left: Back porch.

6322 NORTHWOOD (1940)

This home on Northwood was one of very few one-story houses that Charles Dilbeck designed. It features Dilbeck's signature crooked brick.

Above: 6322 Northwood.

Left: The back.

6322 NORTHWOOD

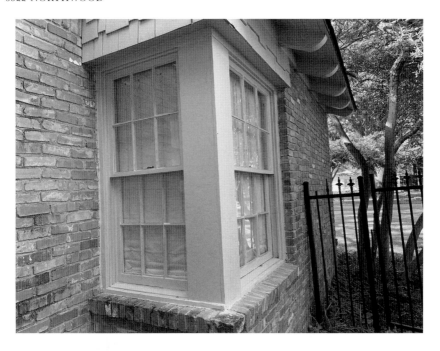

Top: Windows. *Bottom*: The fireplace.

6043 PARK (**1942**)

As a prime example of Dilbeck's Country Ranch–style house, 6043 Park features stone instead of brick, which is rare for the Dilbeck houses in Preston Hollow.

6043 Park.

6043 PARK

Top: The outside. *Bottom*: Stained glass.

6132 DELOACHE (1951)

This home was built in 1951 for Malcolm Cloyd for his mother-in-law. His main residence was 6122 Deloache. This is one of few homes Charles Dilbeck built in the 1950s.

The side.

6132 DELOACHE

Round Dilbeck post.

Left: Front door.

Right: Fireplace. *Ellen Hoffman.*

6132 Deloache.

CONCLUSION

As a resident of Preston Hollow on Northwood Road since 2010, I have always been deeply intrigued by its history. So many unique stories were on the verge of being lost forever, and so much fascinating information is completely unknown to most. I was inspired to write this book to share Preston Hollow's unique story not only with residents of Preston Hollow, but beyond. Despite what many think, so many of our historic homes and landmarks are actually still standing, all of which are monuments to Preston Hollow and the people who founded it. The homes from the 1920s and Ebby's Little White House all have such different but amazing stories representing the diverse background of the neighborhood before its development in the 1930s. Ira DeLoache and Al Joyce bought and resold many acres of land, attempting to persuade Dallasites to move to their rural developments, and the neighborhood would never have been what it is today without them.

The original residents of Preston Hollow courageously dedicated their lives moving to the middle of nowhere, during a world war, in order to make the neighborhood what it is today. Entrepreneurs like William Underwood, Claude Ezell and Sam Lobello kicked off commercial business in an isolated area, and other dedicated people—like Dr. Cecil H. Lang, who commanded the project to plant a church in Preston Hollow (Preston Hollow Presbyterian Church), and Kenneth Bouve, who led a day school housed in a gatehouse and chicken coop into what is now one of Dallas's top private schools (St. Mark's)—showed their dedication to their piece of Preston Hollow's history. Probably one of America's best architects in the early twentieth century,

Charles Dilbeck, designed homes in only two cities (with some exceptions), Dallas and Tulsa, and we were lucky enough to receive many of these amazing homes in our neighborhood. Preston Hollow's two mayors, Joe Lawther and Mart Reeves, courageously led a town with no taxes and little resources for six years, from 1939 to 1945. When the township was beginning to fail, Dallas mayor Woodall Rodgers proudly accepted Preston Hollow into his city and constructed schools and paved roads in the area, leading to the development of the neighborhoods north of Royal Lane in the 1950s and 1960s and many commercial businesses choosing to locate themselves in the Preston Hollow area.

As time goes on, a new group of people has moved to Preston Hollow, with many of them building new homes. Those residents who continue to be proud of and deeply love Preston Hollow have enhanced the amazing community feel of the neighborhood one hundred years later. The land, the people and the homes all contributed to this gem situated right in the heart of one of America's greatest cities.

BIBLIOGRAPHY

Adams, Billie S. Telephone interview with author, June 17, 2020.

Allen, Tom. Interview with author, October 9, 2020.

Archer, Marguerite. Interview with author, February 11, 2021.

Barbee, Elizabeth. "Preston Hollow Joined Dallas More than 70 Years Ago." *Preston Hollow Advocate Magazine* (March 24, 2016).

Bishop, Barry. "Dallas Acts Quickly; Hems in Park Cities by New Annexations." *Dallas Morning News*, April 5, 1945. infoweb.newsbank.com.

Boose, Paula. "Dallas in 'The Western Architect,' 1914: Places of Leisure, Etc." *Flashback Dallas*, August 25, 2018.

———. "Neiman's First Suburban Store: Preston Road—1951–1965." *Flashback Dallas*, August 2, 2020.

———. "Preston Royal Fire Station—1958." *Flashback Dallas*, November 7, 2014.

Brodsky, Lael. Interview with author, September 25, 2020.

Brooks, Bud. Telephone interview with author, November 13, 2020.

Caruth, Jo Ann, and Shanna Caruth. Interview with author, September 27, 2020.

Chiames, Chris. E-mail correspondence with author, August 9, 2020.

Coursey, Jack. "Preston Royal Theatre." Cinema Treasures. cinematreasures. org.

Dallas Morning News. "Little White House on Preston Has Stood for Almost Nine Decades." November 23, 2012.

———. "Now the Vogue—the Modern Country Home." October 18, 1931.

————. "Preston Hollow Incorporation Plan Climaxes Weeds-to-Orchids Development." September 24, 1939. infoweb.newsbank.com.

————. "R.B. Stichter, 56, Found Dying in Yard at Home." infoweb.newsbank.com.

Dauwe, Chris. Telephone interview with author, September 13, 2020.

The Department Store Museum. "Neiman-Marcus, Dallas, Texas." Date unknown.

————. "Sanger-Harris, Dallas, Texas." Date unknown.

Dietz, Sally Fryer. Interview with author, August 15, 2020.

Dunning, Tom. Interview with author, January 1, 2021.

Faulkner, Scott. Interview with author, March 7, 2021.

Fix, Barbara. Telephone interview with author, August 17, 2020.

Greene, A.C. "The City of Preston Hollow." *Dallas Morning News*. Date unknown.

Griffin, Laura. "'McMansions' Alter Landscape." *Dallas Morning News*, June 15, 2002.

Grimes, John, and Ellen Grimes. Interview with author, November 6, 2020.

Groves, Todd, and Shelly Groves. Interview with author, September 19, 2020.

Halbreich, Jeremy, and Nancy Halbreich. Interview with author, November 3, 2020.

Hoffman, Ellen. Interview with author, October 4, 2020.

Johnnie J. Myers Transportation Research Center. "Stichter, R.B." Date unknown.

Johnson, Marietta Scurry. Telephone interview with author, August 7, 2020.

Kresl, Lisa. "Ghosted: A 100-Year-Old Strait Lane House Haunted by a Nun." *Preston Hollow Advocate Magazine* (February 12, 2019).

Limón, Elvia. "Dallas Once Had 19 Drive-in Theaters. Now It Has Zero. Curious Texas Explains Why They're Gone." *Dallas Morning News*, April 18, 2019.

Lively, Jack. Telephone interview with author, May 30, 2021.

Maxon, Peter Flagg. "Early Preston Hollow." *Legacies: A History Journal for Dallas and North Central Texas* 14, no. 2 (Fall 2002).

May, Thomas C., and Elenor May. Interview with author, September 4, 2020.

McCormack, Tom. "Preston Hollow Remembered." Unpublished typewritten document.

McCoy, Nancy. Dallas Landmark Commission Landmark Nomination Form for 5310 Park Lane. August 2015.

Melino, Jim. Interview with author, October 30, 2020.

Miller, Jody. Telephone interview with author, August 10, 2020.

Mills, Elizabeth Dickey. Telephone interview with author, October 27–28, 2020.

Moore, Twila. Telephone interview with author, June 24, 2020.

National Oceanic and Atmospheric Administration. Storm Events Database. https://www.ncdc.noaa.gov/stormevents.

Nicholson, Eric. "The Battle for Preston Hollow's Soul." *Dallas Observer*, October 22, 2014.

Nienhueser, Cindy B. Telephone interview with author, August 3, 2020.

Parham, Jo Ann. Interview with author, May 31, 2020.

Parker, Howard. Telephone interview with author, August 17, 2020.

Payne, Darwin. *Dynamic Dallas, an Illustrated History*. N.p., 2002.

Pittenger, Barbara. Telephone interview with author, August 17, 2020.

Preston Hollow. Dallas Historic Aerial Photographs, 1930 Fairchild Survey, October 1930. Edwin J. Foscue Map Library, Southern Methodist University Libraries.

Preston Hollow Advocate Magazine. "The Little White House" (June 1, 2001).

Roberts, Bob. "Preston Hollow Presbyterian Church History." Unpublished document available at the PHPC Library.

Sartain, Charles, and Erica Sartain. Interview with author, September 25, 2020.

Scurry, Richard. Telephone interview with author, August 12, 2020.

Sham, Kristy. Interview with author, July 31, 2020.

Shutt, Nancy Perkins. Interview with author, July 31, 2020.

Siegel, Jeff. "Do-It-Yourself Government." *Preston Hollow Advocate Magazine* (December 1, 2000).

———. "Preston Hollow History." *Preston Hollow Advocate Magazine* (November 1, 2002).

Simon, William R. *St. Mark's School of Texas: The First 100 Years*. Dallas: St. Mark's School of Texas, 2006.

Stansbury, Joan L. "John T. Lively and Bluff View Dairy." Pioneers of Dallas County, February 2, 2018. Dallasgateway.com.

Staubach Gates, Jennifer. Telephone interview with author, September 4, 2020.

Stewart, David E. "The Spirit of Merici." *Continuum*, January 2010.

Sudbury, David, and Holly Sudbury. Interview with author, August 15, 2020.

Temple Emanu-El. "History and Architecture." tedallas.org.

Van Horn, Larry. "Mary Stuart Stichter." Find A Grave, April 19, 2014. findagrave.com.

Walnut Hill Elementary School. "A Walk to Remember with Walnut Hill." dallasisd.org.

Walton, John Brooks. *The Architecture of Charles Stevens Dilbeck*. Tulsa, OK: JBW Publications, 2006.

Wikipedia. "Lone Star (St. Louis Southwestern train)." https://en.wikipedia.org/wiki/Lone_Star_%28St._Louis_Southwestern_train%29.

———. "Morning Star (train)." wikipedia.org. https://en.wikipedia.org/wiki/Morning_Star_%28train%29.

Williams, Jim, and Glenda Williams. Telephone interview with author, June 23, 2020.

Wilonsky, Robert. "An Obituary for a Preston Hollow Landmark Soon to Be Destroyed for 5 New Mansions." *Dallas Morning News*, July 4, 2019.

Wilson, Linda. Interview with author, September 25, 2020.

YouTube. "Sanger-Harris Preston Center Remodel—September 1962." Uploaded by SMU Jones Film, June 24, 2018. https://youtube.com/watch?v=cBZqoDUpwkA.

INTERNET RESOURCES

Dallas Central Appraisal District. dallascad.org.

Dallas North Tollway. ntta.org.

NewsBank InfoWeb. infoweb.newsbank.com.

Preston Hollow Park. dallasparks.org.

Public Records Encyclopedia. clustrmaps.com.

U.S. census, 1940. rootsprint.com.

Zillow. zillow.com.

INDEX

ABOUT THE AUTHOR

Jack Walker Drake has been a resident of the Preston Hollow neighborhood since he was five years old and has always been fascinated by its history. He wrote this book at the age of fifteen. At the time of this book's release, he is an Elder at Preston Hollow Presbyterian Church and attends Trinity Christian Academy in Addison, Texas. Jack also has a lifelong passion for aviation and is in the process of getting his pilot's license at American Flyers at Addison Airport.